To: Pastor Paul Stennett

From: Cameron Hodge

"All things work together for the good of those who love God, those who are called according to his purpose." Ro. 8:28

Love,

By His Stripes

Memoirs of a College Student

Cameron Hodge

WestBow
PRESS

Copyright © 2011 Cameron Hodge

All rights reserved. No part of this book may be used or reproduced by any means, graphic, electronic, or mechanical, including photocopying, recording, taping or by any information storage retrieval system without the written permission of the publisher except in the case of brief quotations embodied in critical articles and reviews.

WestBow Press books may be ordered through booksellers or by contacting:

WestBow Press
A Division of Thomas Nelson
1663 Liberty Drive
Bloomington, IN 47403
www.westbowpress.com
1-(866) 928-1240

Because of the dynamic nature of the Internet, any Web addresses or links contained in this book may have changed since publication and may no longer be valid. The views expressed in this work are solely those of the author and do not necessarily reflect the views of the publisher, and the publisher hereby disclaims any responsibility for them.

Any people depicted in stock imagery provided by Thinkstock are models, and such images are being used for illustrative purposes only.

Certain stock imagery © Thinkstock.

Unless otherwise noted, all Scripture quotations are taken from the Holy Bible, New International Version®, NIV®. Copyright © 1973, 1978, 1984 by Biblica, Inc.™. Used by permission of Zondervan. All rights reserved worldwide. www.zondervan.com. Scripture quotations marked ab are taken from The Amplified Bible. Copyright © 1954, 1958, 1962, 1964, 1965, 1987 by The Lockman Foundation. Used by permission.

ISBN: 978-1-4497-1049-1 (sc)
ISBN: 978-1-4497-1050-7 (e)

Library of Congress Control Number: 2010942837

Printed in the United States of America

WestBow Press rev. date: 3/14/2011

Special Thanks

I thank my family, friends, and my church for their support of this book. Most important, I thank Jesus Christ for allowing me to share my testimony in order to glorify Him and to help set His people free.

Surely He has borne our griefs
And carried our sorrows;
Yet we esteemed Him stricken,
Smitten by God, and afflicted.
But He was wounded for our transgressions,
He was bruised for our iniquities;
The chastisement for our peace was upon Him,
And by His stripes we are healed.

—Isaiah 53:4–5 (NKJV)

Introduction

I have not always been saved, but I am now. Before I knew Jesus, I tried other ways of "coping" with my issues, all of which did not work. I tried several self-help theories and ways of thinking, but they came to nothing. When I met Jesus, and became sincere about following Him, my whole life changed. Jesus makes the difference in a person's life because He is real, and He is the Healer. When I once believed that others did not love or want me, Jesus came into my life and accepted me; He did not reject me. Jesus restored me from brokenness and feelings of inadequacy that made me want to take my own life.

Several years ago, I was raped. I also suffered from other sexual violations that I had kept secret. For years, I harbored the pain and tormenting memories of those experiences. I shared them with no one. Yet when Jesus came into my life, He sent people to help free me from the bondage that held me captive.

I can honestly say that were it not for Jesus, I would not be where I am today: loving life and desiring to help others. I know Jesus is real, and as I share parts of my life with you in this book, I pray that He becomes real to you as well. Not only that, but I also pray that you will open up your life to Jesus and let Him heal your secret wounds.

Contents

Chapter 1	Beginnings	1
Chapter 2	Forgiveness	5
Chapter 3	Purity	39
Chapter 4	Insecurity	47
Chapter 5	By His Stripes	65
Afterword		75

Chapter 1

Beginnings

I sat wide-eyed, watching television late one night. I flipped through channels, trying to find something to watch to pass the time. I came across a program that caught my eye. After watching it for two minutes, my life was changed forever. The words *Feed the Children* were on the screen. A Caucasian man with white hair and a white beard sat on a stool, holding an infant African girl. Their surroundings were foreign to me, things I had never seen. They sat in front of a worn-down, one-bedroom shack, with a patchwork roof made of used material. Flies buzzed around the man and the girl. The picture flashed to dark-skinned children laughing and playing in gurgling water. The camera then returned to the man and the little girl. The man lovingly held this little girl as if she were his own daughter. She seemed innocent and comfortable in his arms. Her little pink dress with white trim stood out against her mahogany skin and luminous black eyes.

    I listened as the man pleaded to the television viewers to send money to help this little girl. He showed video shots of the room where she lived. He explained how she needed clean water, clothing, and an education. As the man continued to speak, the camera focused in on the face of the little girl. The close-up of her face filled the television screen, her skin glistened with sweat. Flies flew around her face, alighting on the small tumor under her dark eyes. I sat on my knees, my face nearly pressed against the television screen. I rested my hand on her face and pretended that I was really touching her. I looked in her eyes as if I were face- to-face with her. Even at my tender young age, my heart ached as I imagined how this girl had never played with a Barbie or ate ice cream on a hot summer day. As the man pleaded for aid on behalf of the little girl, I whispered, "I want to help you." Then her face faded from the screen and the infomercial ended.

With this stark image imprinted on my mind and heart, I crawled into bed and continued to think about the girl. I thought about her for years and still do, even to this day. I wondered what happened to her, if she received the help she needed. Or if, in fact, she, like many other men, women, and children, was left helpless to die in an unfair world of poverty, greed, and apathy.

I was a small child then, but the impact of that moment still affects me today. After seeing that infomercial, I purposed in my heart to learn different languages so that I could communicate with and love those who needed help. I wanted to be able to effectively and sincerely speak love and encouragement into the lives of those who suffered despair and hardship. I determined to learn *at least* two foreign languages by the time I turned twenty-one. I do not know why exactly I chose that age. I suppose because at my young age then, I thought that I could do whatever I wanted by the time I was twenty-one.

I fell in love with language, desiring to communicate in different ways, so I started to teach myself sign language. In elementary and middle school, I checked out sign-language books from the library. Then I closed myself in my room and spent hours learning different signs and phrases. I pretended I was speaking to someone who needed help or guidance and signed such phrases as *I love you* and *I can help you*. My heart filled with excitement at the thought of being able to use my sign language.

In elementary school, I became attached to a girl whom I will call "Jane." Jane suffered from Down syndrome. When the other children ignored Jane, I paid attention to her. We ate lunch together and played together. And I read to her. Sometimes I used sign language with her, trying to connect with her. I loved Jane. She was my first real experience of the love I wanted to share with others. I can still remember what it felt like to hold her hand as we walked. The memories are so clear of us sitting together cross-legged on the floor of the classroom, playing hand games. Then the school year ended, and months passed by before we saw each other again. She did not remember me, but it was okay. I remembered her. She may not have remembered me wiping her dirty nose or tying her shoes, but I did. I still, to this day, remember her face, her hair, and her smile. Sometimes, when I think of her, I can hear her laughter in the corridors of my memories. I will never forget her.

These experiences were innocent. I just wanted to reach out to others. Yet little did I know that God was molding my heart to His will. Little did I know that this desire was God's plan for my life. But first He would have to help me before He could use me to help others.

Throughout my childhood and into my young adult years, I experienced many struggles: depression, attempted suicide, insecurity, unforgiveness, and more.

Yet through Christ I overcame, and am overcoming, them all. God has shown me that sometimes the best help we can give others is not with money or clothing but with encouragement and being able to relate to one another. It is giving someone the testimony that we ourselves have been victorious, that we have overcome the issues that life has thrown in our path. In my opinion, nothing is greater than the testimony of winning the battle of life's struggles. No one can deny your testimony; no one can disprove it, because here you are today.

In John 12, when the Jewish people in the town called Bethany found out that Jesus was there, a large crowd came to see Him. The Bible tells us that people came not only to see Jesus, but the man Lazarus whom Jesus had raised from the dead. The chief priests, who were already planning to kill Jesus, decided to kill Lazarus as well because of what he represented: "So the chief priests made plans to kill Lazarus as well, for on account of him many of the Jews were going over to Jesus and putting their faith in him" (vv. 11–12). Jesus raised Lazarus from the dead, and people wanted to see Lazarus because they had heard the miracle that Jesus did. Lazarus was a living testament to the working power and reality of Jesus Christ, and no one could deny it. When the people saw that Lazarus, who was once dead, now was alive, they put their faith in Jesus. It was Lazarus' testimony that the chief priests hated because it proved Jesus was real. When people saw the truth, they believed Jesus and followed Him. The chief priests didn't want Jesus usurping their self-made authority. Jesus told the chief priests in John 10:37–38, "Do not believe me unless I do what my Father does. But if I do it, even though you do not believe me, believe the miracles, that you may know and understand that the Father is in me, and I in the Father." Jesus proved that He was the Son of God by what He did. A life that gives glory to Jesus Christ, that is a testament to His authority and grace, is powerful. Let Jesus do for you what He did for Lazarus, and let the power of Jesus Christ reign in your life.

As the world has been told and will soon see, the greatest testimony of a victorious life is that of Jesus Christ of Nazareth. He was sacrificed on

Cameron Hodge

the cross for our sins, our hurts, and our struggles. Yet, He rose from the grave on the third day, defeating death, and because He was resurrected, we can be also. The wounds He suffered and the stripes He received from the whips have allowed us to be healed from our sufferings, struggles, and sin. His stripes can deliver and restore us from every difficulty and challenge we have experienced.

CHAPTER 2

Forgiveness

I have struggled to overcome unforgiveness. Everyone at some point in their lives has dealt with unforgiveness. My battles and victories with unforgiveness did not start recently; no, they started when I was a young child.

I lay frustrated, in my bunk bed. The black-and-white television screen softly lit my room as I squirmed and scratched. I was miserable with chicken pox. Over and over again my mother told me not to scratch and to let the ointment heal the bumps. But she was not there, and I began to scratch. As I scratched, the irritation got worse. It became so bad that I began to cry, which awoke my mother.

"Didn't I tell you not to scratch?" she said as she entered my room and flicked off my television.

"I can't help it. It itches!"

"Be quiet and stop scratching, or I will have to tie you down to the bed," she warned.

I said nothing else. I did not move. Once she left my room, I cried more, but silently, so that I would not be heard. My heart was crushed, and so was my trust. As a child, Mommy and Daddy were my heroes. Every time I had a problem, they fixed it. They knew everything and could do anything. Mommy and Daddy were perfect. So I was hurt when Mommy did not make the pain go away but instead became angry at me for something I could not help. Imagining being strapped to a bed with that horrid irritation frightened me. How could Mommy say this? How could I trust Mommy with my issues again?

This is one of my earliest memories of when I began to harbor unforgiveness. As I look back on this incident, it seems very minor in the big scheme of things. Honestly, I would be pretty upset if my child was carrying on late in the night, when I had to be up for work the next morning. I know my mother was not serious when she said this, and I know she only wants the best for my life. But as a young child, I did not understand the ways of the world, nor the thoughts or ways of an adult. As children we only have the capacity to comprehend the world through our limited, innocent minds; therefore, a minor incident like this can have a great impact on a child. I love my mother and my father very much. They adopted my twin sister and me when we were babies and gave us a good life; therefore, when I relay certain memories, it is not to defame their character nor to speak maliciously of them, or anyone else in this book. I could never thank Jesus enough for the opportunities He gave me through my parents. When I share these memories, it is only to show how these experiences affected my life, whether right or wrong.

"Did you pee in the bed again?"

"No," I lied.

"Cameron! I can smell it in your room. Why did you pee in the bed again? Why didn't you tell me when it happened?" asked my mother.

I was so ashamed that I had once again peed in the bed; I was too old for this now. So many nights I had tried to hide that I was still peeing in the bed. I would wash my sheets and clothes late at night so that no one would notice. I was tired of being punished for something I couldn't help, and I felt like no one understood how humiliated I was every time I wet the bed.

Many of us walk around hurting and bound, yet we do not know why. We act and react certain ways and say certain things and we do not know why. We dream things and think thoughts that are not of God, and we do not know why. We don't seem to be able to understand the connection between past events and current behaviors. A lot of these reactions stem from incidents that we have never forgiven or let go of; therefore, they have festered within us. I used to think of forgiveness as words we say and then hope that the hurt goes away. But instead of addressing the pain, we compress it, pushing it into a secret place, deep into a hidden cave under the ocean of our hearts, never to resurface—at least, that's what we hope. We think that somehow, someway, that hurt will eventually dissipate. But in my own experience, the hurt does not disappear.

By His Stripes

But then one day a friend gets a little too close. Like an adventurous, bold diver, he or she finds your hidden cave. Then the hurt gushes, resurfacing more ugly and repulsive than it was when you first buried it.

"Go to your room, Cameron. You should not have done that. You know that when you lie, there are consequences," my father said.

"I didn't lie! I didn't lie!" I stormed to my room, feet pounding the carpet, eyes swelling with tears. I slammed the door behind me, and began to cry loudly as I paced my room, boiling with irritation. That irritation turned to anger, then the anger to rage.

My dad walked into my room. "Cameron, I need you to stop crying. You have to learn that you cannot lie. Lying is not good and you do not want to be a person who lies. You have to learn to tell the truth even if you get in trouble, because you get in more trouble if you lie and your lie gets exposed." My dad was usually very calm with my sister and me, even when we did wrong. But I, on the other hand, was not calm. I was a stirring hurricane ready to take out anyone and anything in my path. He shut the door, leaving me alone. And I snapped.

"No one understands me!" I shrieked. I jumped to my feet and began beating my fists on the walls. I screamed and scratched at everything in my room. "Leave me alone! Leave me alone! I hate everyone!" A high chair sat in my room, which I used for my Cabbage Patch dolls. I threw it across my room as I cried.

"Cameron! What are you doing!" my father demanded.

I rushed to the door to keep him out. "Go away! Nobody understands me! No one! Not even you!"

"What's wrong, Cammy? Why are you so angry?"

"Go away! Can't you see I don't want you or anyone else around? No one cares about me!"

My father spoke softly to try to calm me. "Honey, we care about you very much."

"No, you don't!"

"Can't you see that we love you? We only want what's best for you." I saw the worry in my father's eyes.

"I hate you, I don't believe you!" It was as if the air stood still.

"You hate me?" Tears welled in my father's eyes. "Honey, I love you. You are my daughter."

I said nothing to him; I just stared with raging eyes.

"I'm going to leave you alone now. Please, come talk to me when you are ready."

He pulled the door closed. I stood with my hand clutching the knob, my chest and head pounding. I had never seen my father cry before now. I sank to the floor and wept.

All the hurt that I had experienced and the aggression I felt toward people in my life resurfaced in moments like these. Even if you asked me to tell you what exact incident I was angry about in the past or who exactly did what, I couldn't give you a clear answer. My emotions were so entangled in me that I no longer separated people or incidents, because everyone was the same: They hurt you.

Everyone was subject to do me harm, adults and children. Kids teased and bullied me in school. So when I came home, my parents had to manage a hurt child who harbored unforgiveness. I know it was not easy for them to deal with me, but they still loved me. And because of that, I will be forever grateful for them.

"You're ugly!" a little boy whispered to me as we formed a line to go outside my elementary school classroom.

"Shut up. I am not!" I returned

"You shut up! And you stink, too!" These words were common for me to hear. It was recess time, and I was wearing an outfit that I liked and was hesitant about playing too roughly. I wore a little black jumper decorated with tiny red flowers, accented with red tights and black baby-doll shoes. As we approached the playground, I knew this was going to be another recess in which I would fight.

"Stupid girl!" The little boy yelled to me as he laughed and threw a handful of dirt on my jumper.

"Leave me alone!" I threw dirt back. Then several more little boys circled around me and hurled insults at me. All I could do was cry. I didn't understand why they picked on me. I ran and hit one of the little boys, breaking the circle, creating a playground-wide chase after me. It was hot and I ran, sweating and scared. Out of breath, and light-headed, I stopped. As the boys rushed to me they formed another circle, laughing. The boy I had hit previously began to punch me.

"Hey! What are you all doing over there?" yelled a teacher from across the playground. The circle dispersed and the whistle blew to end recess. I lined up with everyone else, feeling dirty, hot, and emotionally crushed. As we walked inside, the little boy punched me one more time. I told my teacher, but she didn't do anything to help me or to punish the bullies.

I suffered a lot of pains and hurts that no one knew about. I had a great deal of anger and rage, so much hurt and confusion. I was tormented daily in my mind about who I was or was not. I was anguished about wounds I bore. Even at a young age, I entertained thoughts of suicide. Death and hopelessness were frequently on my mind. I kept a mental list of the wrong things done to me, and the wrongs I had committed. Unforgiveness controlled me for years.

As a child and youth, I lashed out. I went into rages. I pulled out my hair, threw and kicked things. I said that I hated people and told them not to touch me. I screamed that no one understood my turmoil, and in reality, no one did. Unforgiveness is poison, and for years I was toxic.

People hurt and abuse other children and adults; they use and misuse us. Through all of this, we as young adults must understand that we have a way out of this turmoil, and that way is Jesus Christ. You do not have to walk around any longer in torment, because Jesus is more than able to set you free. He breaks the chains, links, and tentacles of every stronghold with which Lucifer tries to keep you bound in your misery. When I was raped, I became lost in the hurt, embarrassment, and sheer horror. I was an angry, bitter mess that only God could fix.

It was late, and the drive-through of the fast-food restaurant where I worked, was moving slowly. Then a stranger pulled up to place an order. As he pulled to the last window where I worked, I greeted him.

"Hello! How are you?" I chimed.

"Wow, you are very beautiful. What is your name?"

"Cammy." I smiled, and then he told me his name. He appeared only a bit older than me, so I thought his comment was innocent.

"You should come and hang out sometime with me and my friends," he suggested as I handed him his food.

"Yea, that sounds cool, I guess."

He came into the restaurant several days the following week. He seemed to always come around when I was working and asked my coworkers about me. As a teenager, I thought nothing of it. In fact, I was flattered, but I had no idea what I was getting myself into. One night, I was released from work early and he was there. He said that a few people were getting together at his apartment, so I decided to join them.

"Where do you live?" I asked, as I slipped into the car.

"Not too far, just walking distance from here." The car smelled of marijuana and alcohol, so I cracked the window to get some fresh air. Something inside me told me I had made a mistake and that as soon as I got the chance, I needed to run.

As we approached the apartment, I became more alarmed, but said nothing. What if I was overreacting? How could I escape? I didn't drive. Where was I?

He opened the door and we stepped into his apartment. He locked the door behind us. The air in this place was thick with the smell of fried chicken and weed. I even saw the blunt wrappers on the table, along with the bags of weed beside them.

"You want a hit?"

"Nah, I don't smoke."

"Okay." He chuckled and left me alone in his living room.

"Hey! Where are your friends?" I yelled back to him. "When are they coming?"

"They aren't coming. It's just you and me."

And he was right, no one ever came. No one came to save me from the rape, devastation, and confusion I felt that night. No one was there to hear my cries of "No!" and "I don't want to do this!" No one was there to rescue me from my naiveté, insecurity, and low self-esteem that enabled me to go a place with a man that I shouldn't have gone. When it was over, I tried to act like I was okay, but I wasn't.

Looking back, I understand from my experience what preachers mean when they say that sex creates soul ties. Souls ties are attachments our souls make to the souls of others when we become intimate with them, whether sexual or not. Even though I was not saved, I remember what felt like chains binding me to an unseen monster. Honestly, I believe Heaven cried for me that night. All the beauty of life became ugly, and from that day forward I was locked in deep mental bondage that I could tell no one. I believed that if people knew I had been raped, my image of "the good girl with a good head on her shoulders" would be ruined. I would be seen as the imperfect, impressionable, insecure girl that I really was.

I kept my rape a secret for many years, a secret that nearly killed me. I had decided not to tell anyone because I was afraid that no one would believe me. I feared not being sympathized with or understood. I was terrified of losing relationships with family and friends—those people who thought I was a normal person would find out just how screwed up I was. Yet the greatest motive for shutting my mouth was the pain it would cause those who loved me. I imagined the look on my parents' faces, and in my mind I heard my mother and father crying and felt their hurt that their little girl had been abused and mistreated. Images of my father's heart breaking because he was not able to protect me tormented me. I can count on one hand how many times I have seen my dad cry. I knew he would cry if I told him. I envisioned hearing my mom's voice as she wept because she would give anything to trade places with me and take the pain I had suffered. My heart became heavy thinking about the distress my mother would suffer as she would try to help me cope. I could not allow any of this to happen. Yes, my thinking was wrong; however, that was how I felt. I did not want anyone else to suffer because of something I had experienced. So I kept my secret.

When I look back on those years, I can't help but cry because I wish I had known Jesus then. I wish I knew then what I know now: that Jesus heals all and fixes all. There are those of us who carry around sexual abuse, shame, depression, thoughts of suicide, and more, but we never tell anyone, and that is wrong. That is a form of bondage. The Bible tells us in 2 Peter that we are slaves to whatever has mastered us. Any ungodly thing that rules our lives makes us slaves, telling us what to do, how to think, and who we are. Jesus is the only worthy One to be Lord over our lives, not our struggles. In Romans 6, the Apostle Paul explains that when we follow Christ, we are no longer slaves to sin but to righteousness: "I put this in human terms because you are weak in your natural selves. Just as you used to offer the parts of your body in slavery to impurity and to ever-increasing wickedness, so now offer them in slavery to righteousness leading to holiness. When you were slaves to sin, you were free from the control of righteousness. What benefit did you reap at that time from the things you are now ashamed of? Those things result in death! But now that you have been set free from sin and have become slaves to God, the benefit you reap leads to holiness, and the result is eternal life. For the wages of sin is death, but the gift of God is eternal life in Christ Jesus our Lord" (Rom. 6:19–23). This means that when we submit to Jesus, His love, and His Word, He places us in a right relationship with Him and God the Father. We don't have to keep doing things that we are ashamed of, because we have become slaves to righteousness. We don't have to continue to be slaves to unforgiveness, which displeases God and corrupts our lives. The slavery that the Apostle speaks of when he says "slaves to righteousness," is not slavery as we think. When we hear the words "slavery" or "slave," we imagine whips, chains, beatings, being degraded, and living like animals. However, being a "slave to righteousness" means that our lives are now controlled by our right-relationship with God the Father and His son. Within this control is the best for our lives, and treasures we couldn't even dream of. We no longer live for the desires that destroy our lives, because we have become entwined in the majesty and lordship of Christ. Yes, God does have commands for our lives. But in those commands and boundaries, is our ultimate freedom. He tells us to do certain things so that we can have the best life, and be free from situations and issues that can hinder our lives. We don't have to be slaves anymore to any sin, struggle, or situation that hurt us in the past. If we have the faith to believe we can succeed-we can! If there is a struggle that has control over our lives, we can pray to Jesus and ask Him to help us. We can ask There was something that I believe my faith taught me: there is a difference between struggling and willingly remaining in something. I believe that a struggle involves two or more opposing forces that are battling over something. Therefore, for example, if I am struggling with an addiction then that means I myself am trying to get free, but the stronghold of the addiction is trying to keep me bound. Here, we see that two opposing forces are fighting to have control over my life. How can we say we are struggling with sin, or an issue, if we are on the same side as that issue? If I am willingly in addiction, then there is no struggle, because I want to be there; I am not fighting against anything. I had to ask myself: am I really struggling, or do I want to be in this situation? You may be struggling with an addiction right now, or something else, *but keep fighting*. Don't let your problem over take you. You can win this fight because you already have the victory through Jesus. This is not the end for you. Like Jesus told the people right before He rose Lazarus from the dead: "This sickness will not end in death." So, to reiterate the Words of Christ, I say to you: Your fight to overcome will not end in your defeat when Christ is on your side. You will live. I found that reading the Bible, which is God's Word, showed me the areas in my life that I needed to improve. It showed me right from wrong, and if I really wanted to remain in my struggles (Hebrews 4:12-13). Honestly, sometimes it's more comfortable to stay in our current problems, because the process of being healed from those problems can be painful. I have realized in my own life that I was masking my sin, my problems, and my issues by saying I was "struggling" with something, when actually I did not want to stop doing what I was doing. Struggles are not easy and they can hurt us very badly. Yet, we know that we have the victory over every battle with sin: "But thanks be to God! He gives us the victory through our Lord Jesus Christ" (1 Corinthians 15:57). We may not see the victory, but our salvation guarantees that we are victorious: "In fact, this is love for God: to keep his commands. And his commands are not burdensome, for everyone born of God overcomes the world. This is the victory that has overcome the world, even our faith. Who is it that overcomes the world? Only the one who believes that Jesus is the Son of God" (1 John 5:3-5). The Apostle Paul tells us in Romans 8:37 that "in all these things we are more than conquerors through him who loved us." Jesus loves you and I in such a way that I cannot even express; there is so much love in His heart for us. He does not want us to suffer the consequences for our sin, and miss out on the life designated for us. Jesus doesn't want you to miss out on enjoying life, or on a relationship with Him. We all have done wrong (Romans 3:22-26). Especially me. So don't feel condemned, because you can make it, you are special to Jesus and He is in love with you. I am not saying all of this to point fingers at anyone, if I were to ever point fingers, they would all point to me. We just have to be honest about our lives. As we live daily by the Spirit of Christ in us, we have to reject everything, which would try to master us and take our lives and even our identity. Whoever Jesus created you to be, is who you are. All of Jesus' thoughts towards you are lovely. You were so special, that He died for you, just so you could live a better life. Sometimes we are so deceived by the Enemy that certain sins and struggles become deep-seated in us. We begin to believe "it is just who we are," or "we were born that way." I am here to tell you that this form of thinking is wrong. This is slavery, and we have become slaves to our issues if we think this way. Alcohol had me enslaved. Now, my addiction didn't look like the "normal" addiction. What I mean is, people couldn't see my addiction to alcohol, because I hid it very well. I was never drunk to the point of vomiting to a point that people could see, or unable to walk or to function. Nonetheless, I was still drunk. The alcohol had such an enormous influence on my life because a drink was the first thing I thought about when I became depressed or upset. It got so bad, that I began to sneak alcohol. My mind became hooked on it and it scared me, because I had seen what alcohol abuse and addiction did to other people. Lives have been ruined, families broken and finances destroyed because of drug and alcohol addiction. I was slowly spiraling silently into that same destruction. My alcohol addiction got so bad that my mind began to talk to me, and tell me that I needed alcohol. Every time I got down I would hear my mind saying "Go get a drink," and many times I did just that. I was addicted, and no one ever knew, and I thought I would always have to live with that addiction tormenting my mind. I believed that I could never be free from alcohol and that I would forever live with those voices and those urges, and my ultimate submission to alcohol. Self-mutilation was another issue that had me enslaved. Much like the alcohol addiction, I turned to cutting on myself whenever I felt I had done wrong, or when I got upset. Cutting on myself was my way of punishing myself, or taking my anger out on myself. In my warped thinking, I also figured it was better that I harmed myself than harm others in my anger. Many times as I was cutting on myself crying, I would scream and tell myself that I deserved it. The cutting got so bad, that I knew I had to hide it. During autumn and winter months it was easy to hide the cuts on my arms, because I was wearing long-sleeved shirts. But, when summer came around, it became very difficult. Many times I would wear long sleeves in seventy-degree weather to hide my arms. If I couldn't do that, I would watch how I positioned my arms in certain ways when I was around people, or I would bring a sweatshirt or light jacket with me to cover my arms, when I needed. I was a slave to my issues and I am not ashamed to admit that, because I am not a slave any longer. As you see in this book, many struggles I faced controlled my life. They determined everything I did and as a result, I developed a mentality of bondage. But we must understand that this is only deception from the Enemy to keep us bound in our struggles, and to hinder us from seeing the truth that will set us free. Some of us come to a point where we get tired of fighting and we just accept defeat. Addiction, depression, thoughts of or attempted suicide, and much more are some of the traps Satan sets for us. He finds our weaknesses, or bents, and preys on them, using any number of tricks to enslave us. Jesus can liberate *anyone* from any and all sins, and troubles. We just have to be willing to take the steps to be transformed. Sometimes this is not easy. I thought rape, fear, suicidal thoughts, low self-esteem, addiction, insecurity, and a slew of other issues had mastered me. But my faith in Jesus brought me out, and now I serve Him, out of my love for Him, because He first loved me.

One of the ways that Jesus helped me was through confession. 1 John 1:9 tells us that if we confess our sins, God is able to purify us from everything that has us bound, which keeps us from having a true relationship with Him. With confession comes freedom. The Devil never wants you to confess your sins, issues, and hurts to someone because he knows that with exposure, freedom is sure to follow. Jesus sent me a friend who shared a similar testimony. When she came alongside me and told her story, I told her mine. Instantly I felt a freedom I had never experienced before. I finally realized I was not alone, that I would not be rejected and shunned by all if I told my story.

Laura was one of the greatest gifts that God could have ever given. Up until that time when I met her, I had never had a friend like her. The beginning of college was rather lonely for me, even though I excelled in my course work. I met Laura through mutual friends and quickly knew that she would be a friend for life. She was everything I wanted to be. I longed to have the confidence and the faith in Jesus that she had. When I looked at my shattered life, it refreshed me to see how she lived her life. Honestly, I didn't understand why she reached out to me, or why she desired to be my friend. In my eyes, I wasn't much of a friend; I was so broken that I wasn't much help to anyone, let alone someone who knew Jesus the way she did. I was nervous the first night she asked me if I wanted to hang out. How was I supposed to act?

"Turn that up; that's my song!" she said as we rode in my car to the restaurant. I looked at her.

"Really, you like that?" I asked

"Yeah, girl! That's one of my favorite artists!" I didn't even know who this female gospel singer was on the new CD I had bought—my first and only Christian CD at the time. I didn't have much money to buy many new CDs, so I listened to this one all of the time. This new acquaintance seemed cool, and I was starting to think that this could actually be a true friendship from God.

A few moments later we arrived at the restaurant, and when we sat down, we began to talk about everything: guys, clothes, music, school, and God. I didn't know Jesus like she did. So I listened as she explained to me how much she loved Him.

"I don't know how I could live my life without Jesus. He is the real reason that my life has changed."

I sat quietly, nodding in agreement, but in reality, I couldn't relate to her. My relationship with Jesus was not that strong.

"So," she continued "What's going on with you?"

I leaned on the table with my arms crossed. "Nothing, why?"

"Don't lie to me. What is it that has you so hurt on the inside?"

"Look . . . I've made a lot of mistakes, and I've been through a lot—"

"I understand, but you will never be able to heal from those things unless you confide in someone you can trust. You may not feel comfortable telling me, and that's okay, but you need to tell someone. God does not want you to go through anything by yourself. He loves you too much for that."

I listened to her and as she spoke, I felt everything on the inside of me burn. It was as if I was on fire on the inside. I knew Jesus was speaking directly to me through her.

Laura paused as though considering something important. "I don't usually do this, but I am going to tell you what happened to me. I really believe God wants me to tell you this."

As I listened, I felt every cold place in me begin to melt.

Laura told me how she herself had been raped. Her story was similar to mine.

"God had to heal me from the fear I felt of people. I was scared to let people get close to me. I had nightmares and I was bitter toward everyone, including God," she explained.

My eyes began to water. I couldn't hold it in any longer. "I was raped," I whispered. "I haven't told anyone, and didn't think I could because I thought no one would understand what I had been through. I feel so dirty." When I finally revealed my secret, I felt like chains around my heart were loosening and breaking off.

After hearing my story, what happened to me, what I'd done, and how I hated myself and wanted to kill myself, she just loved me and comforted me. Finally! After years of living in prison, someone came and unlocked the doors. Not only was I free, but someone else was walking with me to help me get used to my new life.

If you are reading this and you are hurting, find someone with whom you can be honest—a trusted friend, a teacher, a pastor. Open your mouth and tell that person that you have been marred. Then let Jesus heal you. I know doing this is hard, and it can seem like the hardest thing to do. But please do it. This may mean life or death, not only physically, but also spiritually, emotionally, and mentally. Help is out there, and the greatest help is Jesus Christ. First Peter 5:7 reads "Casting the whole of your care [all your anxieties, all your worries, all your concerns, once and for all] on Him, for He cares for you affectionately and cares about you watchfully" (AB). That last phrase, "He cares for *you* affectionately and cares about you watchfully" (emphasis mine), is powerful. Jesus has an intimate love and care for you. This verse tells us that we can stop carrying the weight of our burdens, and we can trust Him to carry them. We see in Isaiah 53:3-4 that He carried our grief and our heartache on the cross. Jesus carried our hurts on the cross even when we didn't know Him; even when some of us hated Him. Yet, Jesus loved us so much that He bore the excruciating pain of the cross so that we would know the full extent of His love. His love displayed on Calvary dealt with all of our hurt and pain, and enables us to live a life of freedom. The Bible tells us in verse 5 the punishment that He suffered, in our place, brought us peace. We should be living in peace, not in misery and chaos! If Jesus was resurrected from the torture of the cross, what is stopping us from being free from the agony we face? If we serve the One whom death couldn't even hold, what can hold us?

A major lesson I have learned is that unforgiveness is a spirit that does not travel alone. It brings the whole gang with it: insecurity, bitterness, rage, anger, malice, depression, regret, isolation, suicide, and more. When people do horrid things to us, we typically act out with those feelings. I have had countless times of depression. There were nights when I would go to bed crying and wake up crying. My unforgiveness caused me to isolate myself from people because I figured that if one person hurt me, everyone else would, too. I started to cover up who I really was and secretly disdained those who I thought did me wrong.

I was alone again, as I was quite often, and I was hurt. A friend of mine had responded to me in a way that I didn't like. To this day, I cannot remember exactly what that person had done. But knowing the state of my mind and spirit then I probably twisted what she said because of my own internal struggles, as a result of my unforgiveness. Unfortunately, those struggles linked to unforgiveness caused me to go to the extreme often.

"I'm so tired of being rejected," I screamed to myself. I hated me; everything about me was disgusting in my eyes. As I sat in my room, I began to have dangerous thoughts that I knew only came from Satan. But I was so hurt, I didn't care. "I want to die; I don't want to live in a world where I am ignored!" I threw my pillow across the room as I screamed. "Why am I so rejected! I want to kill myself. Maybe if I die people will notice me!" I rose and fumbled through the dark apartment into the kitchen. I grabbed the steak knife and hurried to my room and shut the door. I lay in my bed that night wrestling with thoughts of suicide. Satan and the Holy Spirit were battling for my life it seemed. I began to slowly cut my wrists and then stopped, crying and asking God to help me. But I kept hearing Satan's voice telling me I was nothing and that I should die. "No! I can't die. I can't die. There has to be more! Jesus help me!" I cried. I felt hopeless. I knew that if God didn't come through that night, my family and friends would awaken the next morning to news of my death. They would find me cold and lifeless in a pool of my own blood. Dead by my own hands.

For the next week, I slept with that knife under my pillow, not for protection, but battling suicide. I thank Jesus that He kept me from taking my own life. After that next week, I received prayer for my suicidal musings. Jesus met me in prayer by telling me that He loved me and that I didn't have to live in the prison of rejection any longer; I was accepted and not rejected. Moments like these pushed me to be saved. I knew someone else needed to take control over my life, because I couldn't handle it.

I received Jesus Christ as my Savior and Lord during my sophomore year of college. On this night just before I made my decision to invite Jesus into my life, someone tried to force himself on me sexually, but fortunately he stopped.

I had invited an old friend over. I really liked this person, even though we weren't on the best of terms. I wanted him to like me, to notice me, but my intention was not sexual. However, I shouldn't have had a male over that late, so I should not have been surprised by what happened next.

"Stop, I don't want to do this!" I said over and over, trying to push this young man off of me. He was forcing himself on me and I was scared. I started screaming, pushing, and kicking. "No! No! I don't want to do this!"

He didn't say anything. He ignored my cries. It was as if something had overtaken him and he wasn't the guy I had known before. In my mind I was asking Jesus to save me because I didn't want to be raped—not again. Even though Jesus was not my Lord then, I called Him anyway because I figured if anyone could help at that moment, it would be Him. Then suddenly, the young man froze. He gaped at me wide-eyed, a scared look on his face.

"Cammy! Do you see what I almost did? Do you see what almost happened? I have to get out of here!" It was as if Jesus stepped right in and stopped the whole thing. Jesus saved me that night, in an instant.

Though the aggression stopped, I felt disgusting and debased. I lay in my bed and I cried for what seemed like hours. I needed Jesus to make me whole again and to heal me from all of the bad experiences I had. I needed Jesus to purify my life from every bit of sin that I had committed and all the wrong that had been done to me. I wanted my life to end. I cried out to Jesus, because I was humiliated at how I had made wrong choices. I was in anguish at how tethered and worn I was from mental, spiritual, and physical mistreatment. In a simple prayer, I sincerely gave my life to Jesus that night.

Salvation was the first step, now I had to begin to let God touch the sensitive places within me. I had to let God not only save me but shape me. He had to shape me into the woman He destined me to be by healing my wounds and restoring the broken places in me.

I didn't like people touching me, especially in ways that I thought were inappropriate, like hitting me on my shoulder or in a way that seemed threatening. Even if they were joking, or if the gesture was harmless, I would get upset.

"Hey, Cammy!" my friend ran up from behind me and hit me playfully on my arm.

He was smiling, happy to see me, but I was angry that he had touched me. "Don't touch me like that!"

"Woa, woa! What's wrong with you?"

"I don't like people touching me; don't touch me."

I didn't like my personal space being invaded. He was an intruder to me; I didn't care how nice this friend was, or how long I had known him. By this time in my life, as a young adult, too many people had touched me too often in the wrong ways. Too many people had intruded in on my life long enough. What I didn't realize in this situation was that I was still dealing with residual feelings and emotions caused by the rape. I was holding on to unforgiveness and bitterness I had toward other people who I believed had violated me either physically and/or emotionally, whether intentionally or not. I believe we are healed only as much as we have forgiven others. If we cannot release the people from what they have done to us, then we cannot be released from the issue. That sin still stains our lives, and according to Matthew 6:15, God the Father cannot forgive us because we have not forgiven others. I had so much unforgiveness for the person who raped me and for the other people who came before and after him who hurt me and misused me as well. Forgiving others can be the hardest step. Salvation is more than the Father forgiving you of your sins; it is also about Him delivering you from the effects and strongholds of sin done by you and wrongs done to you.

Right after salvation life was still hard, because it took time for Jesus to work on me. I still exploded on people and I still raged. I was hurt and torn on the inside; I felt battered and alone. My wretchedness and the chaos I felt was still evident in my responses to people.

Numerous times my mother would try to reach out to me, but I wouldn't let her in; I wouldn't let anyone in. I was so bound by past hurts that everyone was a potential threat.

"Cameron, you know that I love you, right?" she would ask me.

"Yes."

"I hope you know that. Even though we do not always agree, I love you." She was so sincere, as she was many times with me. But I was unbreakable.

"Okay, I understand." I was cold and closed off from people, even when they were genuine. I was determined that I was going to do everything in my power not to let people get close enough to hurt me. So I let them hear what they wanted to hear, but I didn't let them get inside to see who I really was.

As I walk through my memories, I can truly see how Jesus has changed my life, because certain memories show just how low I was in my turmoil. Yet, when I look at my life now, and how I act now, I know the credit goes to no one but Jesus. He truly changed me to who I am today; and He is still molding me into a better person.

"Shut up, don't say anything else! You won't walk all over me anymore!" I screamed. I was in one of my rages again. I don't remember exactly what happened, but I remember being cursed out and belittled by a best friend that I loved dearly.

"You're a mess-up. You always mess things up. You're stupid, Cammy, and you've always been a screw-up and you always will be."

We stood in my apartment, my eyes burning with tears and my heart crushed. How could this person who said that they cared about me, talk to me this way? How could someone in the same breath say "I love you" and then curse you? It was all lies, and I was tired of being lied to. I was tired of being cursed out. Where was the value in friendship? Love was nothing to me in that moment. Love wasn't real; it was all lies.

"Shut up! You don't know me! You don't know what I've been through! Don't you talk to me like that!" I began to beat the walls in the living room as I screamed.

"You're crazy, Cammy, just crazy!" my friend yelled back at me.

In that instant I ran into the kitchen. As I reached for the steak knife on the counter, I fell onto the dishwasher, slicing my toe and leg. I got up quickly and ran to my friend and put the knife in her face.

"You won't hurt me again!" I yelled at her "You won't misuse me again! Don't touch me! Don't curse at me. You will make me do something crazy!"

Everything she had done to me, every hurt I had suffered because of her had exploded in me in that one moment. She said nothing but looked at me with disdain and mockery in her eyes.

"You won't do it," she said.

I screamed at her, dropped the knife, and ran out of the apartment. I dropped down on the steps and watched as my "friend" walked out of my life. My head was pounding. My bleeding foot and leg were throbbing. I sobbed as I slumped on the steps, watching the trickle of blood from my foot and leg.

Thank God, I no longer react like this. When others say or do hurtful things, I try not to hold on to it or hold it against them. Because Jesus Christ lives within me now, I no longer desire to hold on to hurt. It feels good to give it to Jesus. I honestly turn to Him now to help me deal with my issues.

The world would try to make me think my recovery is attributed to other things. I bought several self-help books, and looked online for information to help me deal with my issues. I bought one book that specifically focused on managing anger. It was a good book, but it didn't help. Daily we were required to read about how anger affects our lives and even study some of the root causes for the anger. Moreover, I was supposed to write down how I was feeling every day and even some reasons why I thought I was angry. The book didn't work for me because I needed a human being beside me; someone saved who could show me the love of Jesus. Self-help tips and tricks may work for some people, but it didn't for me. I needed the love of Jesus; I needed the power of God through human touch and encouragement. Actually, the anger-management plan the book advocated only served to frustrate me. I needed more than mere words; I needed a divine touch from Jesus. We all do.

I have seen people get through some struggles without Jesus, but they can never walk in true freedom spiritually without Him. What I mean is, we can never have a true relationship with Jesus and experience the best life He has for us without Him working in our lives. You see, at times I thought I had beaten my rage because I would go months without blowing up. But every so often the Enemy would show just how much control I really had: none. The root of the issue was not rage. Rage was just the fruit produced by the root of unforgiveness in my life. I remember a time after I was "good and saved," I went into a rage and ended up driving to a different city in the country. I do not know if I planned to hurt myself or what. But I remember the rage, because once again, a close friend had done me wrong, or so I thought. And this "wrong" joined the huge mound of unforgiveness that I had carried around for years. She was in reality being open and honest with me. My friend was trying to help me and give me constructive criticism. But even that constructive criticism was something that my insecurity, bitterness, and inferiority complex could not handle—all a result of my unforgiveness.

"Cammy, you were wrong for what you did. You know I love you, but I have to be honest with you."

"Oh, so you have an issue with me, too, right?" I snapped

"No, Cammy, you know I love you, sis, but you were out of line."

"Shut up! Forget you, too! Nobody understands me!" I slammed shut my cell phone and I shouted as I pounded on the steering wheel. I had just been through a drive-through window right before this incident, and I threw all the food out the window. I was livid—again—and I just drove for miles outside of my home city into another city. It was late, and the farther I drove, the foggier the night became. I sped past cars on the narrow back roads. I didn't know where I was, and I soon became frightened because the fog thickened so that I could barely see the on-coming headlights of other vehicles. As I began to slow down the car, I cried. I decided that didn't want to die; I didn't want to do anything crazy. I realized that my insecurities and unforgiveness had made me overly sensitive to take constructive criticism from a caring close friend.

Author R. T. Kendall wrote something very powerful in *Total Forgiveness* that began to change my life. In his book, Kendall wrote that one should pray that God would help him or her to forgive. He also explained that we should pray that God would forgive the person who offended us and ask God to bless them as if they had never done anything wrong to us. This biblical principle has changed my life, and I began to pray for the people who had hurt me.

But to be honest, forgiveness at this level was hard for me to do in many cases, because I felt like God was letting people off the hook for what they had done to me. I thought that everything I had dealt with, every hurt and pain I had endured would be invalidated and forgotten. In my mind, I thought that all of my anguish would never be acknowledged. But from what I have learned, that is not what real forgiveness does. It does not just sweep our feelings under the rug. By God's grace and the power of the Holy Spirit, forgiveness means that we release the person who offended us, so that we can be released, and then Jesus can heal us. Jesus will not invade our lives; He will not touch what we will not let Him touch. He is a gentleman, and He never forces His healing. It is to our advantage that we be willing to cast our cares on Him and let Him heal the unforgiveness in our hearts. Jesus Christ wants us to willingly come to Him, out of surrender and love. Jesus said "Come to me, all you who are weary and burdened, and I will give you rest. Take my yoke upon you and learn from me, for I am gentle and humble in heart, and you will find rest for your souls. For my yoke is easy and my burden is light" (Matt. 11:28–30). Jesus is humble and gentle. He does not condemn us or beat on us for our struggles. He is loving and gentle with our hurts. He lovingly calls us to Him to wipe our tears and fix us up again. Remember when you were little and you would cry to your mom or an older female when you had a "boo boo?" You would ask Mommy to blow on it or kiss it to make it feel better. When she did that, all the pain seemed to leave. Then she would put a Band-Aid on the injury and lovingly send you on our way. I picture Jesus like this with our hurts that we bring to Him, except He really does make the hurt go away and He himself heals our wounds.

Jesus understands our pain. "For we have not a High Priest who is unable to sympathize with our weakness, but we have one who has been tempted in every way, just as we are-yet was without sin. Let us then approach the throne of grace with confidence, so that we may receive mercy and find grace to help us in our time of need" (Heb. 4:15–16). As we see in God's Word, Jesus was tempted in every way. Jesus had to face every possible hardship and temptation. Even the problems that we have never experienced, He has. Jesus is gentle because He sympathizes with our hurts. He can relate to us on every level of struggle. He has true empathy. When we run to the arms of Jesus, we find rest. We can take a deep breath, dry our tears, and rest in Him.

During the Last Supper, Jesus told the disciples of His coming death and resurrection. As He spoke Peter questioned Jesus about what He was saying. Jesus revealed that as much as Peter claimed to love Him, he would deny Him.

"My children, I will be with you only a little longer. You will look for me, and just as I told the Jews, so I tell you now: Where I am going, you cannot come.

"A new command I give you: Love one another. As I have loved you, so you must love one another. By this everyone will know that you are my disciples, if you love one another."

Simon Peter asked him, "Lord, where are you going?"

Jesus replied, "Where I am going, you cannot follow now, but you will follow later."

Peter asked, "Lord, why can't I follow you now? I will lay down my life for you."

Then Jesus answered, "Will you really lay down your life for me? Very truly I tell you, before the rooster crows, you will disown me three times (John 13:33–38)!

As sincere as Peter was, Jesus knew His disciple would betray Him. The Twelve were very close to Jesus. They were around Him when He slept, ate, cried, laughed, and worked miracles. If you look in John 15, you will read how Jesus explained that because the disciples were so close to Him, they no longer had a master-servant relationship. Rather, they were His friends and everything that God the Father made known to Jesus, Jesus made known to them. "I no longer call you servants, because a servant does not know his master's business. Instead, I have called you friends, for everything that I learned from my Father I have made known to you" (John 15:15). Jesus had an intimate relationship with His disciples, including Peter. Yet, Peter denied that he even knew Jesus after Judas betrayed Jesus and handed Him over to Jewish chief priests to be eventually crucified.

The night that the Son of God was arrested by Jewish officials, Peter was seen by several people who recognized him as a follower of Jesus. When asked if he was one of Jesus' disciples, Peter denied Jesus.

Meanwhile, Simon Peter was still standing there warming himself. So they asked him, "You aren't one of his disciples too, are you?"

He denied it, saying, "I am not."

One of the high priest's servants, a relative of the man whose ear Peter had cut off, challenged him, "Didn't I see you with him in the garden?" Again Peter denied it, and at that moment a rooster began to crow (John 18:25–27).

How many of us have been betrayed by those who say that they love us? I think Peter really did love Jesus, but his fear gripped him in a way he never would have imagined. Sometimes, even when people love us, they are still capable of hurting us because they are human and fallible, just like we are. We are all susceptible to the same struggles and fears. Jesus was well aware of how Peter would deny Him, yet He still ate with Peter, walked, and talked with him, and considered him a friend. Peter denied Jesus during the most excruciating time of His life, yet Jesus was still motivated by love to forgive Peter. In John 21, we see that Jesus clearly forgave Peter and asks Peter to help spread His Word and love. Jesus loved Peter past his wrong and did not hold the denials against him.

If we are honest, sometimes we do not want to forgive others for the hurt they've caused. We get comfortable in unforgiveness, and we get comfortable in wallowing in our pain so that it becomes familiar. We can get to the point where to even think of forgiving someone is more painful than holding on to the hurt. Some of us are scared to find out what it is like to live in the freedom of forgiveness. I had to be honest with myself about this: I was all about holding on to what people did to me, whether I showed it or not. But I was only hurting myself.

When we think about some of the most horrible things that happen to us, it is difficult to think of forgiveness. I didn't want to forgive the man who raped me. I thought that forgiving him would be letting him go scot-free for what he did. I also had been so used to living in bitterness; I couldn't comprehend a life without it. It seemed impossible because there was always someone who had the potential to hurt me.

The only way that we can learn how to walk in the fulfillment of true forgiveness is first to know the ultimate Forgiver—Jesus Christ of Nazareth. So let us take a brief look at His teaching about forgiveness. Jesus told a parable of the unmerciful servant in Matthew 18:21–35, which gives us a clear picture of what true forgiveness is and how God feels about it. More importantly, we see the repercussions for someone who is unforgiving.

Then Peter came to Jesus and asked, "Lord, how many times shall I forgive my brother when he sins against me? Up to seven times?" Jesus answered, "I tell you, not seven times, but seventy-seven times.

"Therefore, the kingdom of heaven is like a king who wanted to settle accounts with his servants. As he began the settlement, a man who owed him ten thousand talents was brought to him. Since he was not able to pay, the master ordered that he and his wife and his children and all that he had be sold to repay the debt.

"The servant fell on his knees before him. 'Be patient with me,' he begged, 'and I will pay back everything.' The servant's master took pity on him, canceled the debt and let him go.

"But when that servant went out, he found one of his fellow servants who owed him a hundred denary. He grabbed him and began to choke him. 'Pay back what you owe me!' he demanded.

"His fellow servant fell to his knees and begged him, 'Be patient with me, and I will pay you back.'

"But he refused. Instead, he went off and had the man thrown into prison until he could pay the debt. When the other servants saw what had happened, they were greatly distressed and went and told their master everything that had happened.

"Then the master called the servant in. 'You wicked servant,' he said, 'I canceled all that debt of yours because you begged me to. Shouldn't you have had mercy on your fellow servant just as I had on you?' In anger his master turned him over to the jailers to be tortured, until he should pay back all he owed.

"This is how my heavenly Father will treat each of you unless you forgive your brother from your heart."

What stood out to me in this parable was the difference in the amounts owed to the king and to the unmerciful servant. The unmerciful servant owed the king ten thousand talents. In today's terms that is several million dollars. The other man owed the unmerciful servant 100 denary. This is today's equivalent of a mere few dollars. This was crazy to me when I read this story. How is it that a man can be so unforgiving of someone who owes him a few dollars, when he owed a king several million, yet was set free from the debt? As we reflect on this parable, I believe God asks us the same thing: "How is it that you cannot forgive your brother or sister, when I have forgiven you *all* of your sins?"

There is nothing that anyone could ever do or say to us that merits unforgiveness. Of course, the world would tell us differently, but this is why we must not conform ourselves to the world's system of thinking and feeling. We must be transformed by the renewing of our minds which means that we have to let Jesus' point of view guide our actions and mold our lives (Rom. 12:2). Walking in the true forgiveness of Christ is supernatural. It has to be supernatural because it is by His grace that we are able to forgive. We, in our own fleshly minds and emotions, cannot do it on our own. You may ask: "What about rape victims? What about abused children and women? What about family members of homicide and racism victims? How can you write in this book that these offenses, afflictions, and more have to be forgiven?" I write this because it is the truth. It is the Word of God. I can be honest and say I did not want to receive this Word when I heard this, because I have been through things that I thought were unforgivable. But I was wrong. God can forgive the worst diabolical sin that we could ever commit. The King of Kings and the Lord of Lords forgives us of every minuscule and titanic sin we have ever committed and could ever commit. He sent the ultimate sacrifice, Jesus, so that we could walk in total freedom and forgiveness in Him.

Just like the unmerciful servant did not comprehend, some of us do not see that it was because of forgiveness from God that our debt to Him was canceled. How is it that we cannot cancel someone else's debt toward

By His Stripes

us? Essentially, if we don't forgive others, we are putting ourselves in a place higher than God, and that is wrong. If we do not forgive others, God will not forgive us our sins.

To the world this is foolish thinking! But the Bible says, "For the message of the cross is foolishness to those who are perishing, but to us who are being saved it is the power of God. For it is written: 'I will destroy the wisdom of the wise; the intelligence of the intelligent I will frustrate.' Where is the wise man? Where is the scholar? Where is the philosopher of this age? Has not God made foolish the wisdom of the world?" (1 Cor. 1:18–20). The truth is that the wrongs people do to us do not compare to our sins toward God. The very idea that a man died so that we could walk in the freedom of forgiveness is foolish to many! We cannot use reasoning, fact, and philosophy to comprehend this kind of love. As complex and as brilliant as God the Father created the mind, it cannot understand or make sense of the type of love God the Father has for His children, and the extent of the love Jesus expressed when He was crucified for us. Many do not believe that Jesus died on the cross for their sins and that is their loss. Yet, "for since in the wisdom of God the world through its wisdom did not know him, God was pleased through the foolishness of what was preached to save those who believe" (1 Cor. 1:21). We cannot know God by using just our human reason and thinking. We need faith in the cross in order to open up the door to know God the Father and His Son.

During the time of the Apostle Paul, the young church of Corinth was dealing with a lot of social pressures. In his first letter to the church of Corinth, he encouraged and strengthened the church with the power of the cross. Paul knew that wisdom and eloquence and lofty thinking were not what the people needed to stand against the attacks on their Christian walks. They needed the message and power of the cross on which Christ was crucified.

"And so it was with me, brothers and sisters. When I came to you, I did not come with eloquence or human wisdom as I proclaimed to you the testimony about God. For I resolved to know nothing while I was with you except Jesus Christ and him crucified. I came to you in weakness with great fear and trembling. My message and my preaching were not with wise and persuasive words, but with a demonstration of the Spirit's power, so that your faith might not rest on human wisdom, but on God's power" (1 Corinthians 2:1–5).

Paul stressed that it is only because of Christ and His crucifixion that we are saved, and that we can walk in complete wholeness and in the power of the Holy Spirit. It is in the power of the cross where we find our strength to overcome life's obstacles and stand with Christ. No matter what pressures befall us, if we believe and trust in the truth that Christ died and rose again for us, we always have the assurance that we walk in victory.

I saw in my own life that I began to truly walk in the power of forgiveness and in its liberty when I truly received Christ in my heart, and He became the Savior of my life. Through the love that Christ showed me in my life, I realized that I didn't have to hold on to what people did to me. People who hurt me were no longer in debt to me for doing me wrong, and I was no longer in debt to anyone. Jesus' love began to fill every void, and every empty part of my life that I believed people had stolen from me. Salvation wasn't designed to just keep us from suffering the penalty of sin and wrong; it was designed also to give us a rich life, full of the possibilities, blessings, liberty, and love God has for us.

The Word of God is true. According to 2 Timothy 3:16 it is God-inspired and God-breathed. Therefore, when David wrote this psalm, he did it under the inspiration of the Holy Spirit.

"Praise the LORD, my soul; all my inmost being, praise his holy name. Praise the LORD, my soul, and forget not all his benefits— who forgives all your sins and heals all your diseases, who redeems your life from the pit and crowns you with love and compassion, who satisfies your desires with good things so that your youth is renewed like the eagle's. The LORD works righteousness and justice for all the oppressed" (Psalm 103:1–6).

When God forgives our sins, He does so much more than erase our debt; He begins to heal our wounds, both physical and spiritual. Jesus said in Luke 5:31 that He did not come for the healthy but for the sick. If we hold on to unforgiveness, we are sick and need to be healed from that spiritual disease. Our lives can then be redeemed from the pit of bondage, and we can be renewed and satisfied, and live productive, fulfilling lives for Jesus.

I can relate to David when he says in Psalm 38:4–6:

"My guilt has overwhelmed me like a burden too heavy to bear. My wounds fester and are loathsome because of my sinful folly. I am bowed down and brought very low; all day long I go about mourning."

Some of us have carried shame and guilt for years. We live with the weight of past devastation on our backs, but we pretend like we are okay. I know I did. That is why it is important that we walk fully in the forgiveness and the love of Christ.

God's willingness to forgive us our sins and to help us become great men and women is a gift. It is a gift of His love, yet many of us refuse to accept it. The Bible says in 1 John 1:9 that if we confess our sins He is faithful and just and will forgive us our sins and purify us from all unrighteousness. The word *righteousness* means "right-relationship or right-standing." Therefore this verse means when we confess our sins and God forgives us, He can cleanse us of everything that hinders us from being in a right relationship with Him. I have seen people accept the forgiveness of God for things that most people deem unforgiveable. One night, a friend of mine came to me in confidence and asked me about God's forgiveness. He said he wanted to be saved, but didn't know if God could forgive him for something that he had done. You see, my friend was a member of a well-known gang here in America, and several years prior to our conversation, he had murdered someone. As we talked, I heard the overwhelming guilt and sorrow my friend was experiencing because of the killing. I calmly told him, "God forgives murder, and He can forgive you. He loves you." That night my friend, a gang member, gave his life to the Lord. A relationship with God allows Him to begin working on us and take out everything in us that harms our lives. As God does this, we become thriving, productive, and loving people to our societies, communities, and even our own families. We become better people-great people.

I was talking to a close friend one night about something that God showed me during prayer—I was still holding on to unforgiveness. God told me also that I could not have any secrets with people. Meaning, I could not hold anything against someone in my heart. I had to be transparent with my feelings.

I explained to my friend that I was confused; I thought I had forgiven people for the wrongs done to me.

"I think I am okay, I have forgiven them: family, friends, coworkers . . . everyone."

"Well, from what you told me earlier, you haven't forgiven them Cammy," said my friend.

"What do you mean? How can you say that?" I knew the seriousness of unforgiveness. I knew how God felt about it; if we don't forgive people, God cannot forgive us. When I heard this, I was alarmed.

"Cammy, you haven't forgiven them because their character is still tainted in your eyes."

I was taken aback. It was like a ton of bricks hit me in my chest. How could I still be holding on to unforgiveness? As I think on it now, I realize that I had not been walking in forgiveness. Once people had done wrong to me I believed their characters were shot. What I mean is, after I had claimed to forgive them, I still saw their marred characters. For instance, I still closed people off to guard myself from further hurt, or I responded tersely to them. I acted like this because of what those people did in the past and I still saw them as they had treated me in the past. If people told me they cared about me, I said I cared for them, too. Yet in my mind I would think, "Yeah, right, you only care when it is convenient. You do not care about me. If you did, you would not have done what you did." On the inside, I thought of the last several times that person wounded me. I held people's wrongs against them and pretended that everything was okay. I was wrong for doing that. It is scary to think about where my soul would be right now if God had taken my life during those moments. He is so merciful.

Do you know Proverbs 18:8? It reads, "The words of a gossip are like choice morsels; they go down to a man's inmost parts." I like this verse because this is how I think unforgiveness works as well. Unforgiveness gets down into a person's inmost part, our heart. This is why Jesus tells us at the end of the parable of the unmerciful servant that we must forgive from the heart. The heart is the seat of everything about us; it is a reflection of who we are as the Bible tells us in Proverbs 27:19, "As in water face answers to and reflects face, so the heart of man to man" (AB). The Lord tells us in Jeremiah 17:9 that "The heart is deceitful above all things and it is exceedingly perverse and corrupt and severely mortally sick! Who can know it [perceive, understand, be acquainted with his own heart and mind]" (AB). The heart affects how we act, talk, think, and live. So our hearts need a lot of work, and that is a job only for the Most High God. We all have a lot of issues that could and do contaminate our hearts, and it is hard to be who God called us to be with the junk that we have built up in us. The great thing about this is, God does desire to work on us and mold us, to remove the junk, but we have to be willing to let Him. Forgiveness is more than just lip service; it's a change of heart. We can alter our actions for a time, as if we have had a change of heart in the area of unforgiveness, but after a while, what is really in our hearts will show.

As I said before, unforgiveness affected my mind and actions. Every time someone tried to get close, I remembered how I had been hurt in the past. I had the mentality that most people could not be trusted because in the end, they will hurt you.

This kind of thinking resulted in years of ungodly actions toward others. It was hard for me to tell the truth, even about simple things, because the spirit of fear had taken hold over my life because of my unforgiveness. I could not be honest with people about what I needed or the way I felt for fear of losing friends or being ridiculed, belittled, or flat-out hurt like I had in the past. I had not forgiven the people who had, in my eyes, treated me this way. If someone asked me if I needed help, I would say no. Not because I did not need the help, but I would rather have gone without the help than to be honest and say I needed it. Why did I do this? I lied because in the past when I needed help and asked for it, I believed I was treated wrong in the responses. For example, someone may have offered to give me the help I asked for but attached strings to it, or the person would put me down for even needing help. Instead of getting the mercy and love I expected from those helping me with a need, I felt like I was a burden. I had not forgotten those who had hurt me in the past when I needed help, so the hurt and fear was still there years later.

Many times, the response I received from people in little things like asking for money, or a ride somewhere created some of my unforgiveness. It hurt me when I would ask for a ride and people would sigh, scoff, and give me twenty reasons why it was an inconvenience but they would "sacrifice to help me out." Many times I would tell the person not to worry about helping me, because I was so beaten by the time the conversation was over, that I didn't desire the help. It is humbling to ask others for assistance, and when people aren't humble in their responses to you, it can crush your feelings.

I did not lie in certain situations to be malicious, but to protect myself. In reality, my lying only made things worse. When people found out or "discerned" I was lying, my character suffered: I looked like a liar because I was lying. Then as I was being scolded for lying, I would think in my mind, "Don't you see why I cannot be truthful?" It got so bad that sometimes I could not even be honest with wanting a glass of water. I was living under a demonic stronghold. I developed the attitude of "I can do it myself," and I would not even let people help me with small things.

I knew I had a serious issue, when one night a close friend was giving me a ride home, as she frequently did. As we were walking toward her car, she asked to carry my guitar for me. I told her no that she did not have to because I could carry it.

"Cammy, for real, let me carry the guitar for you. You have a lot to carry already, let me help you. You look tired anyway."

"No, I'm fine. I don't need your help."

She then asked me again. "Cammy, just let me help you." Again I told her no. Because of my stubbornness and the strongholds that bound me, I carried the guitar *with* her, both of our hands holding the case handle. This was ludicrous, and God spoke to me and told me I had to deal with that issue.

I eventually let go of the guitar, but I felt beaten on the inside because I had to give in to someone helping me, which implied that I was somehow lacking in some way. But I knew at the time that I was wrong for acting the way I did.

I did not want any help from anybody, and I did not care how much they claimed to love me or just wanted to help me. I was tired of reaching out to others because in some cases, I felt like I was a burden; I was sick of being someone's liability. I didn't want to hear about how much of an issue, problem, or inconvenience I was. Everyone else had hurt me in the past when they helped me, so what made my friend, or anyone else, different?

This is how many people live, needing help but not asking because fear paralyzes them. I lived in fear, in lies, and in distress for years, and God had to clean me out. I had built up many walls, keeping others at a distance. As I got to know some people, I let them in but only to a certain point. Over time, the walls appeared to come down; however, they were still there. I knew they were there because when people came alongside me when I was in need I went into attack mode. This was because I thought that their help was going to cause me pain or humiliation. I surrounded my feelings and heart with an electrical barbed-wire fence with five deadly Rottweiler's and three snipers in a watchtower. And just in case someone got past the dogs and snipers, I had landmines, ready to explode at the slightest movement.

"Cammy, let me do your hair one afternoon. You would look so pretty if you took better care of your hair. It's so thick; you have nice hair." My friend held a comb as she spoke. "You want me to do it for you?"

"No, for what? I'm fine like this." I was getting upset.

"Cammy, why do you do that? You have to take better care of yourself."

"I do take care of myself. Just because I don't look like you, doesn't mean I don't take care of myself." I was boiling on the inside. How dare she criticize the way I look or dress?

"Are you about to cry?" She laid the comb down and stepped closer to me, searching my face with her eyes. "Cammy! Why are you crying? Why are you so mad?"

My eyes burned with tears; my hands shook from hurt and frustration. "Why does everyone always have something to say about how I look or how I dress?" I exploded. "I know I'm ugly, and I know I don't look like everyone else or dress like everyone else! I don't want you or anyone else touching me or trying to change me!" I grabbed my purse and stormed out of her house. Why was everyone so critical of me? I already hated me enough; I didn't need other people hating me as well.

I drove my car home, crying and angry. I was sick and tired of people, their mouths, and their input. *It's your fault, Cammy. Maybe if you weren't so ugly people would like you.* Thoughts like these assaulted me as I drove. I felt I had to punish myself for my ugliness and my inadequacy as a human being, and I knew exactly how I would do it.

As I walked through the door of my dorm room, I rushed to my box of utensils and grabbed a knife. I then lay in my bed and began to cut on my wrists.

Nobody likes you. I watched the knife slide back and forth as blood seeped out. The cuts stung and burned, but I didn't stop. I deserved the pain I was feeling. It was my fault I was not accepted. I made myself this way, and it was my fault that I was never what people wanted me to be; therefore, I had to be punished.

I am a sensitive person by nature. Yet, during these inner battles, I was ultrasensitive, far more than I should have been.

My mind used to race as I imagined what people thought of me, or ways they would possibly hurt me. I would have thoughts like "No, don't walk down that street, a man will jump out and harass you." The spirit of fear had gripped my life. I was scared of almost everybody and everything. I was a wreck. All of my unforgiveness, coupled with all of the other issues I was dealing with, were crashing down on me. One particular day, I received a ride from a male coworker.

"Hey, Cam, did you drive today?"

"Nah, I didn't. My car is in the shop right now." I had taken the bus to work.

"You need a lift home?"

"Um . . . sure." I stepped into the car quickly, trying not to draw attention that I was scared to be alone in the car with this man. In two minutes my mind had run through a whole scenario of how my coworker would not take me home, but instead pull over, violate me, and leave me dead in a ditch on the side of the road.

My mind was jacked up—sick. My first assumption was always that others were going to harm me. I needed Jesus to deliver me from the fear of people that held me.

Not only was I afraid of people, but also I would question their words. As people were talking to me, I'd be thinking, "She is judging you as she is talking to you. You know she doesn't think you're worth anything. In a few days, her true colors will show, and you will get your feelings smashed once again."

Every day certain memories would pass through my mind of how people damaged me in the past. My memories would many times turn into horrible fictional scenarios of things that could happen to me. I had bad dreams and tormenting thoughts.

It was late one night, and I lay under my covers scared to go to sleep. For the past couple of nights I had been having bad dreams of men chasing me and trying to harm me. In my dreams, I relived the events of being raped, and sometimes the dreams were worse than the reality of what happened to me.

This night, I heard glass shattering in the other room. Someone was breaking into my house and I was all alone. I jumped out of my bed and stood in my doorway. Slow black shadows moved throughout my house. Then I was hit in the head.

"No! No! No! Get off me! You won't rape me again!" My head was throbbing. I had been hit across the temple with a pistol. I was screaming! I saw his face, and I heard his voice, the same voice that lured me the first time.

"Shut up! Shut up or I'll kill you!" He slapped me, and I cried and right before he slapped me again, I woke up from the dream.

I lay in my bed and I wept. I was scared. I didn't want another person to hurt me again.

But I wasn't bound by just the memories, or made-up scenarios of things that could happen. I also felt the sting of the hurts harbored within the memories. The Enemy will try to use memories to keep us bound, but God is able to renew our minds and erase the memories. Every day I would recount my rape. Every day I would have the same memories of certain people cursing at me and talking down to me; certain phrases would run like clockwork. Sometimes I would be doing school work or talking to a friend and I would hear the voice of someone from the past degrading me.

I would stop whatever I was doing, and get lost in the memory. Echoes of words would swirl and swirl. But glory to God, not only did He rid me of the pain, but also of many of the memories themselves.

Some things God may allow us to remember, but not so that we stay bound in the memory, but so we do not forget from what God has delivered us! We can use those memories to communicate the grace and power of Jesus in our lives because we have changed and we have been healed from those memories and past experiences.

The memories, the old feelings, the grudges, everything was making me bitter and unforgiving. I know I have already mentioned the following statements in this book. However, I feel the need to reemphasize the next few points, so that you truly understand the importance of forgiveness. Moreover, I want you to be able to detect unforgiveness in your life, by me sharing my own. If you take a look at my life, you may see some similarities in your life. Even though people apologized and I told them that I had forgiven them, I never looked at them the same. I was not walking in true forgiveness because I still saw those people in the light of what they did. I still judged them by their mistakes. When I looked at Myra, I saw her impatience with me; when I encountered Megan, I remembered how she left me hanging after I told her I needed ride, and I ended up walking several miles home. I was so wrong, dead wrong. This is not how Jesus looks at us, nor does God the Father. When we as believers sin against God, all He sees is the blood of Jesus that covers us. As Psalm 103:8–12 shows us, God loves us so much. If He forgives our sins and separates our sins from us, how much more should we do it for someone else?

"The LORD is compassionate and gracious; slow to anger, abounding in love. He will not always accuse, nor will he harbor his anger forever; He does not treat us as our sins deserve or repay us according to our iniquities. For as high as the heavens are above the earth, so great is his love for those who fear him; as far as the east is from the west, so far has he removed our transgressions from us."

Most of us do not see forgiveness this deeply. I never did until it was revealed to me. This is the key to why Jesus tells us in Matthew 6:14–15 that if we do not forgive others, God cannot forgive us: "For if you forgive men when they sin against you, your heavenly Father will also forgive you. But if you do not forgive men their sins, your Father will not forgive your sins."

One important lesson we must learn is that along with forgiving others, we must forgive ourselves. Let's face it, there are a lot of things some of us have done and we feel foolish or bamboozled. We can't believe we fell into certain sins, got into certain trouble or even trusted certain people. Constantly, we condemn and bash ourselves about past events and think about how they "should have gone if we would have known." Yet, we must remember that the past is the past. If God forgives you of your past then you should forgive yourself of your past. You are not perfect, and life is not perfect, but we serve a God who is. That's why we have to lean on Him and follow His leading in how we forgive, in order to forgive ourselves. My personal conviction is this: me not forgiving me is the same as not forgiving someone else. For some of us, the hardest person to forgive is ourselves because this means we have to face the reality of who we are. While forgiving ourselves we have to acknowledge that the situation occurred and that we did what we did or were a part of the situation. I am learning how to forgive myself daily, because I realize I do mess up. It would be a shame to forgive everyone else in our lives then, at the end of this life, realize we fell short of Heaven because we failed to forgive ourselves.

My life has changed and is changing because of forgiveness. I am learning now to examine my feelings, thoughts, and motives toward people who offend me. I also look at the reason why I am offended, and I ask myself several questions in order to find that reason. I do this in order to find the root of the offense, so that I do not harbor unforgiveness. Most of the time we as people, especially as young adults, become offended more easily in the areas of our insecurities. For example, if I am insecure about what I wear, I am offended easily when a trusted friend suggests that I wear something that flatters me in a better way. Was this friend trying to hurt my feelings? Most likely not. Were they trying to help me out? Yes, because they love me. So why would I be offended when they made a suggestion like this? Probably because I struggle with affording clothes that make me look nice. And I struggle with being around other people who dress in expensive clothes that I can't afford. In essence, I feel like the outcast, because I don't measure up. So when my friend gives me constructive criticism, I take it as a punch to my efforts to try to look nice. I take my friend's advice as her telling me I don't measure up. See what I mean in this scenario? Sometimes we have to take a step back and honestly question why we think, believe, act, and react the way we do to certain things. I try to do this now, by God's grace in my life.

I also make conscious efforts to be transparent with others so that I do not hold any unforgiveness, even though this is not always easy. Of course, some people still do hurt me, and at times I think I have forgiven him or her. But the sting is still there and I cannot act the same way toward them that I once had. I go to leadership or close friends who know the Lord, and I go to the Lord Himself, to check those feelings to see if it is unforgiveness. I am not perfect, but I can honestly say that Jesus has allowed me to be more transparent, bold, and truthful about what I am thinking and feeling. I am still growing in this area, but God has truly given me more and more freedom in this area. I go to God with unforgiveness daily and ask Him to cleanse me of it so that there is no room for the Enemy to come into my life. This process has actually brought me and God closer because I share my heart with Him frequently, and He has become my best Friend. If it seems like I cannot tell anyone else my issue, I go straight to Jesus, and He comforts, completes, and restores me in every way.

I know it is difficult, and the process of healing hurts, but we all have to go through it. We have to release people from what they have done to us; that debt owed us has to be canceled. Some of us are even angry with God. We may not admit it, or verbalize it, but we are. I was. In our minds we think: "If God was real, why did he let me get abused? Why was I abandoned? Why was I left in poverty? How could God let me become addicted to something? Why was I raped, when He was the One who was supposed to protect me? How could you let Mommy and Daddy mistreat me when you placed me in their lives to care for me? Why is someone always telling me what I won't be? Why did my Daddy leave my family? Why did I have to watch my mother struggle with addiction? There are millions of questions that we pose. Honestly, I do not know all the answers to these questions. I have searched for those answers, because I too posed similar questions to God. Yet, nothing I found ever sufficed. At the end of the day, I still had to deal with my pain. I realized that I may never know why certain things happened, and maybe that was a good thing. No answer to my questions of why and how could ever take away the pain I felt. Therefore, I resolved not to rack my brain figuring out why I went through what I went through. I turned my focused to my God who promised to heal me, even though I didn't understand everything He did. I turned my focus toward being healed. When I began to focus on Jesus, I began to realize that I didn't need the answers to those questions anymore. The love of Christ flooded my life to the point that holding on to debt owed to me was undesirable; it started to become futile and incomparable to love Jesus showed me. His love toward me completed me, and it began to fill the voids that I thought the answers to my questions were supposed to fill. You don't have to fight anymore. The love of Christ has truly helped me to forgive. Will you let His love flood your heart today?

Chapter 3

Purity

The mistakes and unfair treatment of the past can have a horrible effect on how we feel about ourselves. Some situations leave us feeling devalued. We feel as if some of our experiences have lessened our worth as humans.

The *Merriam-Webster* dictionary gives several definitions for the adjective "pure." The definition that explains the word well is "free from what vitiates, weakens, or pollutes or containing nothing that does not properly belong; free from moral fault or guilt." One can say that purity in God's eyes is a state of being totally consecrated and set apart for God in your mind, body, soul, and spirit; and free from any moral fault or guilt because of the blood of Jesus.

All of us have experienced things that make us feel stained, as if we are contaminated. We feel ashamed and guilty. Tarnished. A number of situations can make any man or woman feel this way particularly sexual abuse or emotional distress, especially when caused by someone we love. Sometimes, I believe women deal with this to a much greater degree than do men. This is because women want to feel cherished, unique, untainted, like one-of-a-kind.

"I'm sorry," I said, even though I wasn't sure what I should be sorry about. I was on the phone with a guy-friend who did not treat me well. This night he was upset at something I had done. Even though I don't remember what it was exactly, I remember I had been careless. I had overlooked something that he thought was important. And because of this, he cursed me.

"Cammy, You can't ever do anything right. You're just stupid sometimes."

I cried on the phone. I was blindsided by all of the anger he had toward me. I didn't understand how it had gotten this far, and I didn't understand how he could speak to me this way.

He kept cursing me and yelling. He called me degrading names and belittled me. I was scared, contaminated by the filthy language and the attitude he had toward me. I was supposed to be special; someone he cared for. We were supposed to look out for each other. In this moment I realized I was not as special as I thought I was.

Men and women deal with the stains of their past mistakes, and it can be hard to get to a place of feeling clean and washed. When something comes along to crush those feelings of purity and uniqueness in a woman, she feels as if she is not as valuable or precious as she once was. We see this a lot in young women who have been sexual active, whether voluntarily or involuntarily. Many women struggle silently with not being sexually pure. In the body of Christ, and even in families outside of it, virginity is a virtue. The Bible tells us that fornication, sex outside of ordained marriage between a man and woman, is a sin. Whether or not people stress virginity for Christ's sake or for tradition's sake, many women who are not virgins struggle with not being pure in the way that society and even religion says they ought to be. However, we need to look at purity, not just in a sexual context, but in everything that can contaminate our lives: drugs, insecurity, lying, cheating, cursing, depression, suicide, deceit, masturbation, and more.

Women and men who ponder their imperfections and consider their contamination typically condemn themselves. They live day-to-day with thoughts of how less of a woman or man they are because of things they have done or that have been done to them, sexual or not, that have contaminated them. I heard something in a sermon a few years ago that changed my life and freed me from my bondage about not being pure—not only sexually pure but also pure in regard to my lifestyle and past mistakes. The load of my mistakes constantly pressed on me. Every day memories of the rape played continuously in my mind. Every day certain mistakes I had made in the past would bombard my thoughts and I would feel dirty inside. I thought that I would have to live the rest of my life with my feelings of filthiness and that I could never be cleansed from my past. I felt that I had no hope of a fresh start.

By His Stripes

But then I heard this in the sermon: "When you become saved, in God's eyes you are a virgin. The world will tell you that you are not, but in God's eyes, you are." This was profound! Purity is more than just about sexual virginity, it is about the state of our soul, our spirit, our entire lives! We need to see our purity through God's eyes when He looks at us: When we become saved, we *are* pure. We are no longer contaminated with sin and the world, because we have been washed in the blood of Jesus Christ. Praise be to God! "Come now, let us settle the matter," says the LORD. "Though your sins are like scarlet, they shall be as white as snow; though they are red as crimson, they shall be like wool" (Isa. 1:18).

Salvation restored my purity, because when I started putting my faith in what Jesus said about me in His Word, I began to act like it. His Word transformed my life. The Bible says in 2 Corinthians 5:17 that anyone who is in Christ, meaning makes Him the Savior and Lord of their life, is a new creature. We become a new creature because the things that we once did and suffered are null and void in God's eyes. Those moments have passed away and the new life that Jesus has for us has come. Therefore, salvation showed me that I had a new and clean slate. I no longer had to view myself as the "messed-up Cammy." I no longer had to wallow in my past because in Jesus' eyes, all that stuff didn't matter anymore. He was giving me a chance at living a new life that glorified Him. This new life didn't have to be filled with the mistakes and pain I bore and the sins I committed. This life could be filled with the promises, love, and freedom that Jesus intended for me to have. Now when people bring up my past I simply tell them "I'm not like that anymore, and I don't do those things anymore," and I don't have to feel like a hypocrite for saying that; it is true! Now when people curse at me and treat me unfairly, I have the power to respond in a Christ-like way and keep a high level of integrity. I can love people who hurt me instead of hate them. And it's all because of what Jesus has done in my life.

"I asked for only mayonnaise and lettuce on this burger! And you gave me pickles. I want my money back!"

I looked at the woman, trying to keep my composure as she thrust the sandwich into my hand through the drive-through window. "I'm sorry ma'am, but you seem to have eaten over half of the sandwich. We cannot refund your money," I replied calmly. "I can get the manager if you would like."

"No, I don't want to speak to a manager," she shouted. "I want my food!"

I stepped from the window, and asked the grill crew to make the lady's sandwich over again. Even though I knew she was in the wrong, I didn't want any problems. I handed her a new hot sandwich, and then she opened the wrapping and examined it.

"That's right!" the woman screamed at me as she called me the "b-word." "You better give me my sandwich."

In that moment, I knew I could do one of two things: politely send her on her way, knowing that Jesus loved me and that I didn't have to respond. Or, I could come through the window, curse her out and then get fired. I was saved, and realized I didn't have to act the way I normally would have, had I not been saved. The old me would have cursed her out, and probably knocked the sandwich out of her hand; but not the new me.

"Thank you, ma'am. Have a nice day and come back to see us!" I smiled as I shut the window.

Another day, I was working the drive-through window and a few young Caucasian men rode to the window wanting their food.

"Hey, baby, you gonna give me some free food?" one of them asked as I opened the window to greet them.

"No." I said calmly as I closed the window to pack their food, but I could hear them yelling insults to me. I decided to keep my mouth closed, for the sake of my Christian walk and my job.

"Here you are." I handed them the food

"We need mayonnaise, and we need more napkins," one of the other boys demanded.

I closed the window to retrieve their condiments. Two more times they demanded other things, only to have me running back and forth. I knew they were trying to get under my skin. But I said nothing as they hurled more insults at me because I wasn't saying anything and because I wouldn't give them free food.

"Here you are," I said, giving them the condiments they requested. "Have a nice day," believing that our encounter was over.

As the boys pulled away in the car they all screamed the "n-word" at me. That word was yelled so loudly that the other people in the restaurant heard it.

A few months later, I started having issues with different people at my job who would say and do inappropriate things to me. For several months, I dreaded going to work, because I knew I would have to deal with some comment about my body shape and weight.

By His Stripes

One day, I was filling a bucket with water and soap because I was asked to mop the floors. I was in the back of the restaurant at the sink with another female employee. Out of the blue, she began to ask me questions about my body.

"What size bra do you wear?"

"What?" I looked up from the mop bucket.

"What size bra do you wear? You have nice breasts."

I looked at her for a moment and calmly responded, "I don't have conversations like that. That's none of your business." She chuckled then grabbed my chest. She caught me off guard, and I was mortified that my coworker had the audacity to do this. I was upset and told one of my managers, but nothing happened. Nothing ever happened, so when other incidents occurred when I was violated on the job, I said nothing. These events and many more made me feel nasty and weighed on me. I wanted Jesus to take away every filthy feeling in me.

If you have been tainted and scarred and you want true purity in every part of your life, if you want to be free, receive Jesus Christ as your Lord and Savior. The blood that Jesus shed on the cross cleanses us and purifies us. We are no longer who we were before Christ; now we are only who Christ has made us to be. Even though we may not see it, and we still fall short of the glory of God, He sees us as the finished product. God sees us as who He always destined us to be. Hallelujah! "So from now on we regard no one from a worldly point of view. Though we once regarded Christ in this way, we do so no longer. Therefore, if anyone is in Christ, he is a new creation; the old has gone, the new has come!" (2 Cor. 5:16–17).

With every strike of the hammer that forced the nails through His hands, with every open and gushing wound that burned from the heat of the sun as He hung on the cross, with every ribbon of torn flesh and excruciating breath taken, and with every pulsating pain that came from His deep-pricked head as He bore the crown of thorns, there as He hung, was our sin. Not only did He hang for the sin we were guilty of, but also for the wrong done to us. "But if we walk in the light, as he is in the light, we have fellowship with one another, and the blood of Jesus, his Son, purifies us from all sin" (1 John 1:7). "'Their sins and lawless acts I will remember no more.' And where these have been forgiven, there is no longer any sacrifice for sin. Therefore, brothers, we have confidence to enter the Most Holy Place by the blood of Jesus" (Heb. 10:17–19).

Sometimes we try to make ourselves clean. We think if we do certain things or if we act certain ways, we can get rid of the residue of the sin and wrong. A lot of us struggle more with the wrong done to us rather than with the sin we have committed against God. Those mistakes that cost us our dignity, that made us vulnerable to others are the hardest to get over. So we create a facade to try to cover impurity and sin in our lives. We dress smartly to hide the ugliness inside; we use big words and act spiritual so that others will see our intellect or maturity and not our anguish. We try to make ourselves pure, or at least feel pure, by fleshly and worldly ways. Can I be honest about how I tried to convince others of how pure I was? I wore purity rings to try to make up for the grotesque state that was festering on the inside. I was struggling because of past experiences, physically, emotionally, and spiritually, and I wanted a way to make myself new again. That was my motive. I was ashamed of my mistakes, I was disappointed by those who had hurt me, and I wanted to forget it all. I wanted a new beginning, but I was wrong in thinking I could do it in my own self. No purity ring, no long dress, no holy and deep demeanor did anything except frustrate me more.

I wanted my purity of life to be visible to everyone. One day, I decided that wearing a purity ring would convince others, and me, that I really was pure. As I looked over the shiny silver rings with cubic zirconium, I kept telling myself, "This makes me pure. I am pure if I wear this." If I wore this pretty ring, people would ask me what it meant and I would explain to them how I was living for God and that I was keeping my life pure. My pure life would be visible for everyone to see, and if people were convinced I was pure and was living a right life, then I would be convinced myself. In the course of a few months, I lost four purity rings. I honestly do not know how these rings went missing; it was almost as if they disappeared. I believe my losing those rings was Jesus' way of telling me the mentality I had about purity was wrong. Jesus was trying to show me that the only way I could be cleansed from my mistakes was through Him, not made-made objects or human acts. We are not God; therefore, we cannot take God's role. Nor should we attempt to do what only He can do for us. We do not have to sacrifice or do anything to make up for sin and wrong. In fact, our debt is too great. We can never pay it. Remember, it is only God, through salvation and the blood that Jesus shed on the cross, that we have this honor. That is why David said to the Lord in Psalm 51:2: "Wash away all my iniquity and cleanse me from my sin." I found out that Jesus was the only one who could truly, heal me and free me. "If we confess our sins, he is faithful and just to forgive us and to cleanse us from all unrighteousness" (1 John 1:9).

By His Stripes

Currently, my life in this area has done a 180-degree turn. When I mess up, when I do something that doesn't please Jesus, I don't wallow in it anymore. I go to Jesus and ask Him to clean me, believing that He will, and then I move on. I don't condemn myself anymore because I have faults. Jesus loves me, mistakes and all. I no longer try to make myself look a certain way in front of people; I am who Jesus made me to be, whether people like it or not. I am not perfect, and I don't pretend to be, and that's the beauty of it: I don't have to be perfect. By God's grace, I can approach each day encouraged, knowing that my past doesn't determine my future; Jesus does. The old me that was pessimistic, scared, and doubting is no longer there. I don't get depressed about my past anymore. I don't have a reason to because I believe God loves me.

We see that "As a bridegroom rejoices over his bride, so will your God rejoice over you" (Isa. 62:5). This verse made me love Jesus all the more. Weddings are a joyous celebration. Nothing is more beautiful than a bride walking down the aisle toward her future husband. If you have ever been to a wedding, you have probably seen the groom's reaction when he sees his bride. His face is full of love, excitement, and gratitude to marry the woman he cherishes. Many men have shed tears at their weddings because they are overjoyed. Well, that same look a groom gives his wife on their wedding day is the same look God gives us every time He sees us. Our God loves us so much; He looks past our faults and imperfections and sees who we really are. He knows who He created us to be.

I picture God this way: I am at an outdoor wedding. Sunlight dances off the green leaves of the trees. The area is filled with white flowers. White doves flutter and coo. Then I see Him at the altar. Stars twinkle in His eyes, tears well as I come to Him, white flowers in my hand, wearing a flowing white dress made especially for this moment. The perfume of white roses floats delicately on the warm air. Peace and overwhelming gratitude fill my spirit. This is how I believe it is when He sees us. It is hard for us to imagine the Maker of Heaven and earth, the One who spread the sky above the earth like a canopy, loves us like this. As dirty as we are every day with all our sin and all of our hang-ups, God sees us as the stunning bride dressed in white, carrying white flowers and coming down the aisle toward Him. Jesus healed my wounds of impurity by overwhelming me with His love and His thoughts about who I am.

I feel so special to Jesus—because I am. I feel loved and kept by Him—because I am. He makes me feel unique and treasured—because I am. It is the best feeling in the world, and no one can take it away. I know

Cameron Hodge

that Jesus loves me even when I mess up. I know He still cares for me and desires me even when I do not treat Him well. He is so wonderful; I never thought I could feel this way. How is it that I am in love with One I have never seen?

Chapter 4

Insecurity

"Walk with your head up, Cammy," my mother said often. I walked slowly behind her in the store, often with my head down, counting my steps. I didn't like looking people in the eyes, I felt like they could see right through me at my imperfections. If people saw my imperfections, they would not like me; I would be rejected as I had been by so many other people.

A few days later, my mother and I ended up sitting on the steps in our house and talked about how I was feeling.

"Cammy," she began "you can't keep walking around with your head down. You are beautiful and people need to see your beautiful face."

"I don't feel pretty," I uttered as I began to cry. "I feel fat and ugly."

"You are not fat, and you are not ugly. You have to believe that you are beautiful. You have to work on your low self-esteem. There is no reason why you should feel so bad about yourself that you have to walk with your head down. Stop walking with your head down."

Insecurity slips in so easily with life's trials, especially for children. I struggled with insecurity for years, and still do in certain areas if I am not watchful. That is why I have to submit my mind to Christ daily and bombard my thought life with God's affirmations. All of us at several points in our lives have struggled with insecurity. We tend to think it is all about self-esteem and confidence in ourselves. But we, or at least I, have been seeing this all wrong. From what close friends have shared with me, and from what God has shown me, insecurity runs deeper. The root of my insecurity was trust in God, or lack thereof. According to Acts 17:28, it is by God that we live, move, and have our being. What I saw was that I couldn't know who I was if I do not know God, because I would not know who I came from. It is hard for me to trust what we do not know, and God cannot do for me what He wanted because I was still defining myself by everything else except The One who created me. I trusted everything else except God. I realized that in order to trust God with my life I had to have faith in Him.

I had to trust that because my life was in God's hands, He was going to provide everything I needed and that He was going to support me in everything I did that pleased Him. Therefore, when I tried to follow His Word and live the way He wanted, I couldn't be scared of people's reactions nor the outcomes of seemingly unfavorable situations.

"Hello, is this Cameron Hodge?"

"Yes it is. May I ask who is speaking?"

"This is Sandra. We received your application, and we are very interested in having you work with us. We see that you speak Spanish, among your many other qualifications, and we would like for you to come work with us."

I had given my resume to a job-search agency, and had finally received a call.

"Okay, that sounds great!" Finally I got a call for a job opportunity. I was earning close to nothing at the fast-food restaurant. In a good month, I made $600, which rarely happened. My schedule was filled with school and ministry therefore, I couldn't work that much.

"What is the job?"

"You will be working in customer service, speaking Spanish."

"Okay, that sounds pretty good. What are the work hours, how much is the pay, and where is the office?"

"Our office is located about thirty minutes from your city. The job will start you off at $600 a week, and you would work from eight a.m. to five p.m. Monday through Friday."

At first I was excited: $600 a week was incredible to me; I was lucky to make that in one month working at the fast-food restaurant. To make that much would have been Heaven for me, since I was nearing the end of my college education. However, when I began to consider how the amount of time traveling and working full time would impact my life in other areas instead of just financially, I knew I couldn't take the job. I was involved with my church and also heavily involved with a campus ministry called *Youth Taking Charge* (YTC). I served on the leadership team at YTC, and I

By His Stripes

believed that God had called me to help college students and young adults. If I took this job, my schedule would be so strained that I would not be able to spend time with my peers and serve in the manner that God desired. Moreover, I didn't have a car, and I would have had to take the bus back and forth. By the time I would have gotten back to my hometown, it would be late and I would miss a lot of YTC and church. The only thing I would be able to focus on would be work and school. Even keeping up with school would be a strain with those working hours, especially since I planned to attend graduate school. Jesus had brought me too far in my life and He had blessed me too much for me to give up ministry and serving people.

"That sounds like a great opportunity, ma'am, but I am sorry, I cannot take the job. It would conflict too much with other things I have going on."

She thanked me for my time and hung up.

My life was dedicated to loving the people that Jesus loved and doing what He asked me to do. Therefore, as much as I needed the money, I couldn't take the job. I refused to give up the dedication of my life to Christ for $600 a week. If I sacrificed for Jesus to do His purpose for my life, I knew He would honor that. A few months later, I ended up getting a job that I loved, that allowed me to share my faith, and help others. Not only did God bless me with a job that I loved, but through this position, I received money toward graduate school.

Jesus would not leave me to struggle and be defeated by life's circumstances after I purposed to follow Him. Jeremiah 17:7–8 says, "But blessed is the man who trusts in the LORD, whose confidence is in him. He will be like a tree planted by the water that sends out its roots by the stream. It does not fear when heat comes; its leaves are always green. It has no worries in a year of drought and never fails to bear fruit." When we trust in God, He will bless our lives. God will protect us and enable us to lead healthy, productive, and fulfilling lives because our lives are in His hands. If our lives are rooted in God, as the tree is rooted by the stream, we will never have to be afraid of lacking anything we need because God will provide for us and nourish our lives. When circumstances arise in our lives that try to destroy us, such as debt, addiction, bad grades, abuse, car problems, failed relationships, or what have you, we do not have to be afraid. As followers of Christ we will be like a fruit-bearing tree, having the confidence that Jesus is in control and we will be able to do and accomplish everything He has planned for our lives.

So what does trust have to do with insecurity? "Trust in the

Lord with all your heart and lean not on your own understanding; in all your ways acknowledge him and he will make your paths straight" (Prov. 3:5–6). When we put our trust in God, we recognize that nothing is bigger or more important in our lives than Him. Because of this, we have no higher authority or power to rule over us or mold us. If we make God our stronghold as David talks about in Psalm 27:1, and if He is our light and our salvation, then we have nothing to fear. He would be the greatest aspect of our lives. As fallible humans, we tend to put our trust in things and people that have influence over our lives. Many people trust their jobs or money more than they trust God. Many people trust spouses or friends more than they do God. Therefore, when those things fail, and they will because they are not perfect, we no longer have the security we once thought we had. This is why insecurity has to do with trusting God when you are saved. If we put our trust and faith in the living God, Jehovah, we can never be put to shame according to Psalm 25:3. Halleluiah! The Lord will never leave us nor forsake us (Deut. 31:6). He is perfect in all that he does: "As for God, his way is perfect; the word of the Lord is flawless. He is a shield for all who take refuge in him" (2 Sam. 22:31).

We serve the God who takes our mistakes, ups, downs, disappointments, and shortcomings and makes them all work for us in the best way. The low self-esteem, I used to deal with began to work for me, because I began to think so badly of myself that I was forced to change when I saw other people who were confident in Jesus. I was convicted, meaning I felt like I was in the wrong for saying that I trusted Jesus' Word but yet I was still walking around feeling like I wasn't good enough for anything.

"I'm so stupid to think that people would actually want to befriend me," I thought as I sat by myself at a college function. *No! Stop, Cammy. You're not going to think like that. If you want to meet new people, get up and meet them.* I pushed myself to step outside of my comfort box and talk to people I didn't know. I met several new people that night who had several things in common with me. Jesus enabled my low-self esteem to work for my good because it showed me that I was not thinking or living according to God's Word. My low self-esteem forced me to put action to my faith and believe that I was somebody because I was connected to God, and that I didn't have to be afraid of rejection. I could be confident in whom I was, and I could talk to people and make friends. People would like me for who I was, and if they didn't like me, it wasn't the end of the world.

As I became more secure in whom I was as a woman of God, I began to pray for people, something I normally would not have done. I would

By His Stripes

pray for people I knew and did not know, and I saw Jesus work through a young woman like me, who at one time believed that she couldn't make a difference.

"Cam! I don't know what to do! I'm so scared!"

"What's wrong?" I asked my friend and coworker.

"My baby has been sick for days now with hives. The doctors say it's the worst case they have seen in a long time. The medication that they gave my baby doesn't work. I don't know what to do."

In that moment, I heard Jesus speak to me, "Go pray for the child." I looked at my friend and said nothing as I tried to make since of what Jesus had just said to me. Was Jesus really asking me to go and pray for a child to be healed? What if I prayed for the child and he never got better? What if I didn't pray the right way and I sounded ridiculous? As all of these questions swirled around in my mind, I came to the conclusion that this situation was not about me; it was about the baby who was in need of a touch from Jesus Christ.

"I will go pray for him as soon as I get off of work; I believe that Jesus will heal your child" I said.

"Thank you, Cam! Thank you!"

My manager let me go home early that day, and I was thankful because I was in anticipation of what Jesus was about to do. I decided to go get a small bottle of anointing oil to use on the child. I had seen many people use this kind of oil when they prayed for others, and so I believed that I should use some, too. A few minutes later, I pulled up to the apartment. I was nervous. I knocked on the door and the baby's father welcomed me in.

"The baby is over here." The father led me into the small sitting room. The two-year-old boy with braided hair and small hands lay on the couch. I could see the ointment on him that was supposed to heal the hives. He slept peacefully, unaware of what was about to happen.

"Let's hold hands," I said as we kneeled on the floor in front of the couch. I knew Jesus was there because I felt Him standing beside me. I was comforted and I knew that Jesus had this all under control.

"Wait." I reached into my pocket for my oil. "Let me put this oil on him." I tipped the bottle over into my palm. I rubbed the oil into my hands and then gently ran my finger across the baby's forehead and his arms. "Okay, let's pray." I grasped the father's hand with my left hand and laid my right hand on the baby's stomach, and I began.

"Jesus, we love You so much. We know that You are a healer, Lord. Jesus, we know that it is not Your will for people to experience sickness, especially not Your little babies. Please, cover this child, and please, take away this illness. Your Word says in the book of Isaiah that we are healed by Your stripes. Your stripes are the marks of the whips that You took when You were sent to the cross for our sins. I pray that the blood that You shed for us covers this child and that he is healed. I pray healing in Jesus' name, and it is so. Amen!"

We opened our eyes and stared at the child. I felt as if Heaven was standing in that tiny room with us, because I felt such a peace, yet anticipation in the air.

"Well, I have to go." I quickly rose to my feet. "Let me know what happens. I will keep the baby in my prayers."

I left the apartment, and for the next few days wondered about the child I had prayed for. I didn't see or hear from my friend or the baby's father for the next few days, and then finally I saw my friend at work.

"Cam! Oh, Cam! I have been trying to get in touch with you!" my friend cried to me.

"What's up?" I said, a little startled.

"My baby—he is healed! Right after you walked out the door the other day when you prayed for my son, he started to wake up. As he was waking up, my baby's father said that he watched as the hives started to disappear right before his very own eyes! My son started playing and laughing like he used to before he got sick! The doctor didn't know what to do, but Jesus healed him! It's a miracle!"

I was elated. As my eyes swelled with tears. I hugged my friend as we praised Jesus together in the fast-food restaurant. I ran and shouted praises to Jesus and the other coworkers and customers looked at me like I was crazy, but I didn't care. Jesus had healed a child! He used me, a nobody, to do His work! I was so honored and humbled that Jesus chose me. Jesus became so real to me in that moment, and I knew I had to stay with Him forever. I knew that if He believed in me enough to trust me with His people, then I was a special woman after all. I didn't have to have low-self esteem and a poor self-image; *Jesus loved me!* From that moment on, I began to pray for people. I would pray for customers in the restaurant, friends, and family. I became confident in who I was in Christ.

"Hello, ma'am," I said one day to a customer as she approached the counter. "How can I help you?"

"I've already gotten my food." Her eyes were downcast and her speech was shaky. "I just need some ketchup."

I handed her the ketchup packets as I studied her face. "Ma'am, are you all right?"

"Well, it's my friend. She has this horrible infection on her leg and she may have to have it amputated, and she is in a lot of pain." Her eyes were filling with tears.

"Oh, I see. Well, what is her name? I will pray for her. I believe that Jesus can heal her."

"Really?" the women's face brightened and she smiled.

"Sure, of course!"

"Well, let me go tell her. We are sitting over there." She pointed to the other side of the restaurant. "I will tell her you are coming over."

"Huh? What? She is here?" I was surprised that the lady's friend was here and that she wanted me to pray for her . . . now. It was a risk. The restaurant was busy and I didn't know how it would look to other customers. But I like risks, especially those for Jesus, so I was up for it. "Okay. I will be over there as soon as it slows down a bit."

When I saw a chance to break free from the lunch counter, I made my way to the other side of the restaurant, where the lady was sitting with her two friends, one of whom had the leg infection.

"Here she is. This woman said she would pray for you." The lady I had met turned to her friend. All of the ladies at the table looked at me with expectant smiles and bright eyes. They were much older than me. I was twenty years old, and they were all in their late sixties.

I hugged the woman who was sick and introduced myself. "I am going to pray for you. I believe Jesus can heal you. May I see your leg?"

"Yes, but it's not a pretty sight, dear."

"That's okay, let me see." She raised her pant leg, and I saw the bandage wrappings and the swollen wound. "Does it hurt?"

"Yes, it does. I can't sleep at night."

"Okay, do you mind if I lay my hand on your leg while we pray?"

"No, that's fine, dear. Whatever you have to do, you can do it."

I looked at the clock, I had already been gone five minutes, and I knew my coworkers and managers would be looking for me, but I didn't care. This was the Lord's work and I had to do what He told me to do.

"Let's hold hands." I bent myself over as I held in one hand the sick woman's hand and placed the other lightly on her leg. The other two women held hands and the one closest to me placed her hand on my shoulder. I searched the area with my eyes and saw that the restaurant was busy. People were everywhere.

Cameron Hodge

"We are ready when you are, honey."

I took a deep breath. "Okay, let's bow our heads and close our eyes. Lets pray." There we were: three Caucasian women and a young African-American girl dressed in a fast-food uniform. We were strangers lifting up the name of Jesus in a fast-food restaurant, praying for the healing of a friend. "Dear Lord, we come to you on behalf of our sister. We plead the blood of Jesus over her life and over her leg. Jesus, Your Word says that you came not for the healthy but for the sick. We believe You can heal our sister, we believe that by Your stripes we are healed. Please, heal her, and please, watch over her, her friends, and their families. Please, comfort everyone connected to her in this time. Please, send your Holy Spirit to work in her life."

We prayed for several minutes, and it felt as if Jesus had come and held hands with us. The air was thick and charged. When we ended the prayer, the four of us had tears in our eyes, and we hugged.

"Thank you, sweetie," said the woman who was sick.

"You're welcome. Jesus will heal you." I looked in her eyes and saw a spark of hope that Jesus had put there. As I hugged the other two women, I told them good-bye and went back to work. My heart and spirit were overjoyed at being able to do what God asked me to do, in spite of my insecurity and fears. The old me would not have been able to do that. But Jesus made the difference in my life

"And we know that in all things God works for the good of those who love him, who have been called according to his purpose" (Rom. 8:28). Hallelujah! He is so awesome! This is why insecurity and trust in the Lord go hand-in-hand. When we trust Jesus, we can be secured in who we are as His children. Then, whatever situation comes our way, we will not waiver. Everything has to turn out for our good! Absolute, perfect security is found in God. No man-made thing or human can give us the security that God can.

Some of my coworkers used to make fun of me because I was a Christian. They would test me to see if I was real, and I had to be strong against the adversity on my job. Many times I remember sitting on the bathroom floor in the stall of the fast-food restaurant. I would cry and pray to God to take me from that job, because I didn't like the way I was treated. I was tired of being talked-down to, cursed at, and disrespected. But Jesus had to keep there, because I had to grow from those experiences. I had to learn to stand strong and believe God, no matter how tough the situation became. Jesus was teaching me to be confident and sure of who I was and Who I served, so that I could handle whatever was put in my path.

One manager in particular used to treat me poorly. Surprisingly enough, she came to me one day in confidence and asked me about church. She said she knew she needed to go to church, yet she had too many issues and wasn't ready to give her life to Christ. I told her that Jesus could deliver and change her if she let Him. Even though she did not treat me in the best way, I still had to let Jesus shine through my life, even in situations that made people turn away from me.

As I arrived to work one afternoon, my manager rushed to meet me in the parking lot.

"Cam, hey! I need you to do me a favor." She tried to hand me something that looked like a lottery ticket.

I backed away from her. "What is it?" I could tell she wanted me to do something I didn't stand for.

"I need you to go buy me a blunt and a nick bag with this ticket right here."

"A what?"

"A blunt and a nick bag. It shouldn't cost that much. You can go to the little gas station right up the road."

I looked at her like she was crazy. Who did she think she was? Moreover, who did she think I was? Did she really expect me to succumb to something like this? She was my manager, and I was her employee. This situation was wrong on so many levels: legally and morally. I had had a lot of issues with this manager in the past. She constantly mocked me and made me do extra work that kept me long after my regular work shift. But this was the straw that broke the camel's back. She knew I was a Christian yet decided to come to me with an insane request like this.

"No way. I'm not doing that. I don't believe in playing the lottery or smoking. It's wrong and I don't stand for that. I'm not getting your blunt or nick bag or anything else." I stood there, looking her in the eyes. She wasn't about to punk me and my Jesus. I may have been a lot of things, but I was no punk when it came to Christ, and I wasn't going to destroy His honor for a blunt and a nick bag.

"Dag, Cam! Why do you have to be like that? I mean, I knew you would say that, but I didn't *really* think you'd say that or not do it. Why do you have to do me like that?"

When she said this God spoke to me, *This is how the world views my children.* People do not really believe what many Christian's say because when they are tested, they are shown to have no true power and they fall under the influence of the world. For example, people can hear us Christians say that we ought to be holy as God is holy, as the Bible says. Yet when others look at our lives, we look like other people who are living ungodly and not in the power and holiness of Jesus Christ. I think, to a certain extent, that the Christian walk has become so muddled and defiled that people scoff at the idea of a true Christian. There is a stigma in the world that most Christians are fake, and therefore do not stand for the Jesus they profess to have. But I am here to announce that there are some true Christians who are serious about Jesus and His legacy. We are not perfect, but we are zealous for Jesus and desire above all else to become more like Him and to glorify His love on earth. Our confidence comes, not from our righteous acts. Our confidence comes from knowing that Jesus is real and living, and it comes from what we know He has done and the hope of what He will do in the future.

For the rest of the time that this particular manager worked with me (she was fired soon thereafter), she mocked me for what I had said that day. She told other workers about how I had turned her down because I was a Christian. But this was okay, because I knew who I was in Christ. I was a child of the Most High God and could stand up to anyone with the confidence that Jesus was backing me.

When we trust in Jehovah, we can walk securely in our identity in *Him*. Acts 17:28 showed me that, the Lord is the reason "We live and move and have our being ..." This means that I can never know my true identity or find out who I truly am without Him.

Psalm 127:1 says, "Unless the Lord builds the house, its builders labor in vain. Unless the Lord watches over the city, the watchmen stand guard in vain." We must understand that unless the Lord has His hands in molding us, everything we attempt to become and do is in vain. *It is nothing.* Only God's Word, what He has spoken and what has come to be because of His Word, will last. "Heaven and earth will pass away but my words will never pass away" (Matt. 24:35). Worldly views of security, and secular ways of "finding yourself," all take the glory away from Jesus in the pursuit of happiness and self-worth. And those ways of thinking will come to nothing for us. The Bible clearly states this in 1 Corinthians 2:6: "We do, however, speak a message of wisdom among the mature, but not the wisdom of this *age* or of the rulers of this *age*, who are coming to nothing" (emphasis mine).

By His Stripes

It's all about Jesus, and it's about what He says and what He thinks and what He has ordained. Jesus is the Shepherd, not the world. It is He who guides us and leads us on the paths that we should go. Glory to God! When we trust in God, we are secure in who we are and in what God has called us to do. Deuteronomy 33:13 instructs us to rest secure in the Lord. David said in Psalm 30:6, "When I felt secure I said, 'I will never be shaken.'" This is the confidence we have in the Lord. When we become secure in the Lord nothing can shake us—no matter what the world or anyone says we can or can't do. As the Bible says in Philippians 4:13, we can do everything through Christ because He gives us the strength to do it.

The security that Christ has built up in me, and is continuing to build, has given me the ability to share my testimony and be a witness. Jesus has given me the gift of foreign languages to communicate His gospel and love to those of different cultures. I have been privileged to see others saved and their lives changed through the working of Jesus Christ in my personal life. He has allowed me to connect with people whom I would be fearful even to approach before, because of insecurity about who I was and what I thought I couldn't do. God has allowed me to speak with people, using French, Spanish, and even my limited knowledge of Arabic. I bought a Spanish-English Bible so that I could learn Scripture in Spanish. Many times I would stand before my mirror preaching to myself and teaching myself biblical concepts and scriptures in Spanish. I would imagine that I was before thousands of people in Spanish-speaking countries preaching the Word of God. By the grace of God, I have been able to speak the truth of the gospel in Spanish to others and see them come to know Jesus as their Lord and Savior! Once, Jesus used my limited Arabic to come into the life of a Muslim man from Saudi Arabia. Our conversation was limited by our rudimentary understanding of each other's language. Yet even in that, Jesus blessed the conversation and this man invited me to spend time with him, his wife and child in their home. Glory to Jesus Christ! It is not because of anything I have done but because of God's grace and the power of His Holy Spirit in my life. I take no credit, and I never will.

I wish I would have known all of this sooner. It took me a long time to get to the point where I actually dug my feet in and trusted God. I always thought insecurity was about not "loving yourself," but that is a lie. As briefly mentioned before, I used to walk around with my head hanging down because I was afraid to look at people. I did not think I was worth much, let alone beautiful. People, especially my mother, constantly reminded me to walk with my head up. I tried to find my security in who

I was in everything except God. I was going nowhere, and all I had was a false and superficial security in worldly things. As a child and then as a young adult, certain experiences made me insecure.

When I was nine years old, I came to school wearing a new outfit. I held my head high because I felt so beautiful; it also helped that the other kids commented on how great I looked. Toward the end of the day, when the class was working on math, our teacher stepped out of the room. After she left, some of the boys in the class began to comment on my chest—I was developing faster than the other young girls in the classroom. Though I was not dressed inappropriately, and I was fully covered, the outfit did not hide my development. Several of the boys in the classroom began to call me names, and one young boy began to touch me on my chest.

"You're breasts are huge!"

"No they're not!" I shouted at the boy sitting next to me. "You leave me alone." The other students in the class began to laugh.

One little boy walked over to my desk. "Let me touch them."

"No! You're nasty. Go away!"

He began to grab at my chest.

I was mortified. I felt degraded and nasty. I ran to the back of the classroom and hid in the coat rack. I cried and stayed there as the other children laughed and made more comments about my breasts.

When the teacher returned, she scolded the children for being rowdy. "Where is Cameron?"

Several children pointed to the coat rack, while others said, "She's hiding in the coat rack."

She came to the back of the room and parted the coats and book bags. There I huddled, sobbing and shaking because my whole world of security had been reduced to few bits of rubble.

As a young adult, there was a time when I hated my dark skin. I wanted to have light skin like all of the other pretty and desired ladies on television. I would watch as "red-boned," women were celebrated in the media. Many of the major male entertainers had beautiful women with light eyes and light skin, prancing in music videos. I wanted to be like them, because I thought that they were the ultimate portrayals of beauty. I became so obsessed with wanting to change my appearance that I started to use bleaching crème on my skin. I saw other women use it, and it made their skin lighter, so I thought it would do the same for me. I was even told several times that I was too dark for some men to date me. So, I thought having lighter skin would make me more acceptable; someone would want to love me if had lighter skin.

My confidence rested in my appearance and not on the Word of God. Had I been saved, I would have known the Word and trusted in it. I would have stood strong against what the other people said because my trust would have been in God and in His Word that says I am fearfully and wonderfully made. So even if other people do not think I am beautiful, I know that God does, and that is all that truly matters. We have to learn not to accept thoughts or ideas that are contrary to the Word of God. If God does not believe something about you, then neither should you.

"You have been working with us for a while now, Cammy, and we think you are a great asset."

"Thanks!" I said as I sat in a meeting with my store manager and supervisor.

"We would like to promote you, but we would like to ask you a few questions to learn more about you." The meeting went pretty well, and they asked me several questions about my life and where I see myself in the future.

"What do you plan on doing after you finish college?"

"Well, I would like to work for the United Nations as an ambassador." This was my desire at this time.

"Okay," said the supervisor.

"Yes, sir, I see myself traveling and engaging myself in political affairs internationally, and helping to fight poverty and hunger."

The supervisor smirked and eyed my manager. "Yeah, you may just want to settle for being a manager here at the restaurant," he said to me.

When he said that, I saw the mockery in his eyes. I saw the Enemy in him. I saw Satan trying to discourage me. I wasn't going to let his unbelief in me stop me from reaching to the stars. This time, I knew Jesus, and I was secure enough in Jesus not to become discouraged because others didn't believe in me. So, I simply laughed at him and the conversation ended there. I didn't have to be insecure about who I was, and I wasn't going to let some person I barely knew have any ungodly influence in my life.

My twin sister and I were adopted at seven-months old. That I was adopted never made me feel inferior to anyone nor insecure about who I was. I actually thought I was special because not a lot of kids shared my story. I praise God for the parents He sent to raise us. I also thank God for the relationship I now have with my natural family. As a child, I always wondered who I looked liked. I loved to study people's faces. I examined every detail of people's looks, because sometimes I thought I would be able to identify my natural mother by seeing myself in her, since I came from her. I believe this is the way that we should be toward God. We should be seeking God to know if we can see ourselves in Him and vice versa. Our goal as Christians should be to get to where we can identify ourselves with God; His attributes should reflect in our lives. That is our identity. The Bible says in Genesis that God made man in His image. So when we look at God, we should see some part of us in Him because we are from Him. Moreover, when God looks at us He should see Himself.

I love to see family members who favor one another. Ever since I was a child this has fascinated me. I always ask people, "Do you look like your mom or dad?" or, "Whose eyes do you have?" I examine people closely: The shape of their cheeks, the color of their eyes and the creases of their smiles, and much more enthrall me. It is intriguing to see how God created people individually yet with similar characteristics, but not so similar that they look exactly the same. Even identical twins do not look exactly the same; they still have distinctive different characteristics. I used to wonder whose hair or whose lips I had. God is magnificent in how He created us, and I think it is a revelation of how He feels about His children and the body of Christ as a whole. Although we are not the same, we all have similar characteristics. You can tell we are in the same family because we favor one another, but you see also that we are uniquely and individually made by God for different purposes. What I mean is, we as believers should have Christ-like characters, though our personalities and gifts may be different. This reminds me of the verses in Romans 12:4–5: "For just as each of us has one body with many members, and these members do not all have the same function, so in Christ we, though many, form one body, and each member belongs to all the others."

I loved it when my parents talked about my birth parents. I loved hearing the story over and over again of my twin sister and I being adopted. My parents told us when we were a very young age that we were adopted. They never spoke badly about my birth parents. I think this is why I had such a desire to meet them one day.

One day my mother told me that my birth father had been born in Puerto Rico. This heightened my desire even more to learn Spanish. I thought, "He could be Puerto Rican, and if I meet him one day, I will be able to speak Spanish with him." But my insecurity caused me to plummet into a complex about my identity concerning this. Because I didn't like who I was, the idea of possibly being Puerto Rican gave me something

By His Stripes

to cherish about myself. When I found out my natural father was born in Puerto Rico, it gave me false confidence in who I was as a person. I told myself, "Finally! I know about a true part of me." Yet, because I was insecure about other things, I started trying to identify with the Latin culture, living a lie that I was Puerto Rican. I lived it; I became it. When I spoke Spanish, people asked me where I was from.

"I am from the United States, but I am half black and half Puerto Rican."

When others told me I could pass as Hispanic because of my dark skin and facial features, I felt such a deceiving completeness. For a while, I really believed this, even after I discovered that my natural father was really an African-American born in Puerto Rico. When I learned this I was crushed. Yet, I was so deep into the deception I had created for myself that I continued to believe something about me that was not true. I was trusting in a counterfeit identity.

Since that time in my life God has graced me, through the loving efforts of my mom and dad, to reunite me and my sister with our birth mother and father and little brother. Because I know who I am in Christ, and am learning more about who I am every day, meeting them was a blessing. It was a blessing not because I was trying to find out who I was, but only to see who else was part of the life that God had given me. Jesus has blessed me to spend time with them and even meet my maternal and paternal grandmothers, aunts, uncles and cousins. They showered me with love and received me as their own. Jesus is so awesome and He is so worthy of all the glory!

How many times have we as believers, and nonbelievers alike, continued to believe things about us that were not true? Even after those lies were exposed? People laughed at me because I claimed to be part Hispanic. They picked on my Spanish because I was not nearly as fluent as I am now. Their ridicule offended me. I wanted to be Hispanic. I wanted to trade everything about me for that little piece of what I called reality. I was so insecure about who I was that I subjected myself to a lie.

The security we get from God is not a lie, but truth. The confidence we receive from God is not prideful because we know who we are in Him. In fact, it is anything but prideful. When we realize our immeasurable need for Jesus and His characteristics to work in us, and when we lean only on Him, it produces humility. The humility comes from knowing that it is not because of anything we have done that we have authority or favor or

Cameron Hodge

gifts or even grace. Every good thing that we will ever become is because of the Lord.

Psalm 139 in the Bible is amazing to me. In these passages of Scripture, we see just how uniquely and wonderfully God made us. We have no need to trust in anything else over a God who "discerns your going out and your lying down and who is familiar with all our ways" (vv. 3). I understand why David was a man after God's own heart. How can we not want to stick close to God when He is so in love with us? God knew David so well, as well as He knows us, too, that David wrote of God: "Before a word is on my tongue, you know it completely" (vv. 4). Meticulously, and with great detail, God knit our bodies and personalities together in our mothers' wombs. The moment when He created us was so intimate, because He designed us with a purpose in mind. Then to seal what He placed in us He breathed into us the breath of life, which is His Holy Spirit. There is no one else on earth like you or me, and there never will be. That is how special you are to God and His son Jesus. David says in Psalm 139:14–16:

I praise you because I am fearfully and wonderfully made;
your works are wonderful,
I know that full well.

My frame was not hidden from you
when I was made in the secret place.
When I was woven together in the depths of the earth,
Your eyes saw my unformed body.
All the days ordained for me
were written in your book
before one of them came to be.

Even though David made wrong decisions and sinned against God, God still loved him and David believed that he was still precious and special to God. David had committed sins against God, especially when he committed adultery with Bathsheba and then murdered her husband (see 2 Sam. 11). Even with the other wrongs David committed toward God, he was secure in the truth that God made him uniquely. That is why he said, "Your works are wonderful and *I know that full well*"(emphasis mine). We should be convinced that we are wonderful works of the Lord's hands. We are beautiful in His eyes.

We all have insecurities, but Jesus will work on those areas. I am thankful that God has given me a security like I have never felt, and He is continuing to build that in me every day.

Where once I stuttered and didn't like to talk to people, because of insecurity, I now help with a college ministry where I speak quite often in front of college students. This is only because of God's working in my life. Moreover, I used to be scared to tell people about my past, insecure because of what family, friends, and coworkers would think of me. But now because of Jesus, I can tell my story freely because of the love Jesus has shown me.

He may take me through uncomfortable circumstances that require me to rest in His security, but I am thankful for them. I truly feel that God accepts me, even when others reject me. He has the last say-so, and the only say-so in my life. There was a time when I thought that no one had my back, but I am honored to have the King of Kings and Lord of Lords at my backside and my defense.

CHAPTER 5

By His Stripes

The rain tapped heavily against the windows of the bus. Everything was gray and the air was cold. I was tired, and I was ready for the bus to pull from the station so that I could go home. The raindrops continued to fall and I watched as people scurried through the depot. I began to think about life, and how I wanted to do more with mine. I began to dream about traveling to different cities and speaking to young adults about the power of Jesus. I saw myself praying for people and encouraging them in the Lord. My mind tossed with my dreams of helping to advance the Kingdom of God, and how to help His people prosper. I saw myself, praying for the sick and the crippled, and Jesus healing them instantly. There were people who could not walk, but after encountering Him, they ran, jumped, and praised Jesus. Those who could not see, cried when they gazed on their loved ones for the first time after receiving healing. I then thought about my children and how I would raise them. I saw myself playing with them on a fall afternoon as we examined leaves and talked about how God could have designed them. I saw my family at the dinner table, holding hands as we prayed over the meal I had prepared and set before them. I imagined my husband and me recounting Bible stories to the children while their eyes lit up at the wonder of Jesus, eager to know Him. After dinner, I saw myself putting my children to bed and we said our prayers together. There they were with their tiny hands clasped, and their little eyes shut tightly as they prayed to Jesus.

I knew Jesus had more for me than a part-time minimum-wage job at a fast-food restaurant. Yet, I knew I had to go through some hard times for Jesus to bring me to the place He would have me to be. I looked at the bus depot through the foggy, wet window. I saw sad and depressed faces. People were coughing and grumpy. Others had blank faces. *These people need to see You, Jesus.* Some people were in wheelchairs and others leaned on canes. I imagined laying my hands on each of them, watching Jesus heal them. "Jesus I want people to see Your glory like that," I whispered.

I spent a lot of time in bus depots and on buses, where I saw homelessness, poverty, and sickness. I saw people who needed a touch from the living God.

The bus shook. I looked to see that the driver had climbed on the bus and was ready to leave the station. As we traveled from the city where I worked to the city where I lived, people got on and off the bus.

At one particular stop, it became clear to me why I dreamed the way I did. As the bus door opened, people began to board. I watched as the first woman, an African-American, boarded. Half of her head was bald, where it looked like she had been severely burned. Her skin was pinkish white on the right side of her head and face. It appeared as if someone had purposely burned her, and my heart hurt for her. I imagined laying my hands on her face and the power of God surging through me, healing her skin and making her whole. I remembered the story of the woman with the bleeding infirmity in Luke 8. The woman who had been bleeding for years touched the hem of Jesus' garment and was instantly healed. I knew that the same Jesus who healed the woman in the Bible, was the same Jesus who could heal this woman I saw on the bus. As the woman with the burn walked by, I said a prayer for her. I felt the Holy Spirit speak to me, *Wait and see.* I wanted to get up and go to her, but the Spirit had more for me to see. Following the woman was a group of eight blind people. My heart burned as I desired Jesus to show His glory on that bus. I wanted to go to them and ask them if I could pray for them. I imagined myself praying for them and touching their eyes, just as Jesus did when He healed the blind. I envisioned them crying and praising God as they gained their sight, while the bus' other occupants sat in awe at the power of Jesus. Then, after seeing the majesty of God, I imagined the other people rushing, pleading for prayer for themselves, families, and friends. Everyone was being healed and delivered. I pictured all of this in my mind in that instant. My hands tingled and my heart raced at the mere joy the power of Jesus could bring.

Just then, I believe the Holy Spirit spoke to me. *This is why you are here. I needed you to see the rejected and hurting.* The Holy Spirit began to impress

By His Stripes

in my spirit that I, like all of God's children, am called to the rejected, the lost, the hurting, and the sick. We are called to the people that seemingly have no hope. We are called to tread the dirty and unknown places. God had ordained us to go to the low places to bring His people out. Jesus commands that we love others, that we display His glory so that others might believe and be saved.

That I didn't have a car was a blessing from God, because I was able to connect with and speak to people I might not otherwise have had access to. As I rode the bus to and from work and other different places, I shared my faith with the other riders and the bus drivers. I told them about salvation and how Jesus had changed my life. Jesus led people to me along the bus routes to ask me questions about Him, and I would pray for them. After a while, my spirit yearned to see someone come to Jesus.

And then it happened.

One day, I met a young woman from Nebraska at the bus stop. She needed money for the bus route.

"Hey, what time does the bus come?" she asked me.

"It should be here in a few minutes."

She raised her hand to shield the sun from her eyes. "I'm not from around here. How much is it to ride?"

"It's a dollar thirty" I said.

She rummaged in her purse and cursed when she realized she didn't have any money. "I'm going to have to go get some money. Where is the closest ATM?"

"Down the road. But you won't make it down there and back in time for the bus; it's too far."

The young woman was upset and soon headed down the road. I wished I'd had the money to give her, but I didn't. Then the Holy Spirit spoke to me several times. *Look in your wallet.* At first, I shrugged it off because I knew I didn't have any money, but after the Holy Spirit spoke the third time, I looked. In there were five quarters and a nickel.

"Hey!" I shouted "I can buy your ticket!" I waved to the young woman and she ran back smiling.

"Thanks! You are so nice. I will pay you back!"

"No, it's cool" From that moment on, she and I talked. She explained how she came to my city and what she was doing. As we spoke, I asked if she was in school.

"Nah, I dropped out. I'm trying to get a job, but I can't go back to school. It's too hard."

"Yes, you can. I believe Jesus can help you. You can do it." Jesus began to allow me to encourage this stranger, who was slowly becoming a friend. As our bus arrived and we boarded, we sat together and continued to talk, sharing our stories. I told her some of my testimony. Then she began to reveal some of her struggles. As the Holy Spirit guided me, I encouraged her. We talked for the whole bus ride. We finally arrived to the bus station and then waited for the next bus to take us to our destinations. I realized that all the while we had visited, we didn't know each other's name.

"Wow, I'm sorry, I forgot to tell you my name. I'm Cammy."

She laughed, because she was as shocked as I was. "My name is Donna." It was interesting to me. Jesus was able to move and have His way and we didn't even know the other's name. That's the power of Jesus.

It was a Friday night and I was on my way to church. Donna was on her way to the mall. I invited her to come to church with me. At first she agreed, but then ended up not being able to go. I was a little disappointed. I was concerned about her salvation because I knew she was not saved. Yet, the Lord told me she would be saved. We laughed and giggled through the bus depot as we talked, and ran to catch the buses. We screamed and laughed at the thought of missing our buses.

"Come on, girl!" I yelled, trying to stop laughing because I was running out of breath. "The buses are about to leave!"

"I can't run as fast as you!" she squealed as we ran and giggled.

We reached the buses and I invited her again.

"Since you can't come tonight, would you like to come this Sunday?" I asked her.

"Yea, that would be cool."

My spirit did flips! I was excited because I knew if she came she would eventually give her life to Christ. We exchanged numbers, I told her I loved her, and we went our separate ways.

For the next two days I was in high anticipation and Saturday wasn't passing quickly enough. When Sunday morning came, I kept talking to God about how excited I was. Church this Sunday was great. The Word of God was given boldly and Jesus was glorified. My whole being was in great anticipation for the altar call because I wanted Donna to be saved. As my Pastor made the call to salvation, no one raised their hands. I looked around, shaking with nervousness. I began to pray that God would prick hearts, especially Donna's. I wanted her to experience the love of Christ.

By His Stripes

When no one raised a hand for salvation, my Pastor asked each of us in the congregation to turn to our neighbors and ask them if they were saved. I slowly turned to Donna.

"Donna, are you saved?"

"No."

"Would you like to be?"

"I don't know, Cam; I don't think I can do it. I have too many things wrong with me."

"Yes, you can," I urged with sincerity. "I am not perfect either, but Jesus is great and He can change you. He can change your life. He did it for me. I will walk this life with you. You won't be alone."

She looked down at her feet.

"If you want," I offered, "I will walk to the altar with you."

She nodded. "Okay," she said, "I want to be saved."

I took her hand and we walked slowly to the altar. I cried with joy at what Jesus had done. A complete stranger, whom I met at the bus stop two days ago, came to church with me and gave her life to Christ. In that moment, I saw that little girl I once was, who watched *Feed the Children*. Yet this time she wasn't in front of the television. No, she was living out that dream of spreading love and helping others. The power of Jesus is real, and in that moment He was glorified when Donna gave her life to Him. All it took was a willing spirit and $1.30.

What is salvation? What comes to mind when we hear that word? Do we think of harsh rules, long skirts, and endless hours of sermons that we don't understand? Or do we imagine tedious hours of study in a book that seems to most of us, as mere words that really don't apply to us? Or do we think of rebuking and scolding from older adults who have no idea about the battles we young adults face today? If salvation is such a glorious event and if it is something that *everyone* should crave and faint after, why do people not want it? Because we do not correctly tell and show what salvation is. Without salvation, I never could have begun to walk in forgiveness, security, and purity. Salvation has changed my life for the better.

One day while strolling, I talked to Jesus. As we spoke, He began to reveal salvation to me. He said, *Salvation is a pursuit of holiness.*

"Lord, what do you mean by that?"

He began to show me through His Word. 1 Peter 1 reads:

"Therefore, prepare your minds for action; be self-controlled; set your hope fully on the grace to be given you when Jesus Christ is revealed. As obedient children, do not conform to the evil desires you had when you lived in ignorance. But just as he who called you is holy, so be holy in all you do; for it is written: "Be holy, because I am holy." Since you call on a Father who judges each man's work impartially, live your lives as strangers here in reverent fear. For you know that it was not with perishable things such as silver or gold that you were redeemed from the empty way of life handed down to you from your forefathers, but with the precious blood of Christ, a lamb without blemish or defect. He was chosen before the creation of the world, but was revealed in these last times for your sake. Through him you believe in God, who raised him from the dead and glorified him, and so your faith and hope are in God. "

We were bought at the price of the crucifixion and were cleansed from our sins by the blood Jesus shed. Our purpose in life is to live our lives for God, and God has commanded that we be holy because He is holy. God wants us to become more like Him so we can get closer to Him and live the fulfilling life He has in store for us. Salvation is deeper than just escaping the penalty for doing what is wrong. Salvation is about pursuing His holiness, His likeness, and the life He has called us to live. Jesus did not die on the cross for us to live struggling lives. He did not sacrifice Himself for us so that we live lives of defeat. I had to understand this. It doesn't matter where you are right now: in a jail cell, on the street, in your room contemplating suicide, somewhere thinking about your next high, living in poverty not knowing from where or when your next meal will come, Jesus can meet you right where you are. The same Jesus that has healed and is healing me, and others, can heal you if you let Him. He can provide everything you need and transform your life. I love Acts 1:8 because it shows me that when we become saved, and the Holy Spirit comes in our lives, we receive power. That means God equips us with the power and strength we need to overcome every obstacle of our lives. Through that overcoming, we become more like Him. The same issues and problems that used to weigh us down and defeat us no longer have control over us. We don't just get saved *from the penalty of sin,* but we get saved *to* a better life. Jesus tells us in John 10 that He came so that we could have the abundant life! A life that is full of promise, and a true second-to-none relationship with The One True God, the Maker of Heaven and earth and all that we see.

God has much in store for our lives. Let this good news sink in! There is more to life than what we see with our eyes. Let's grab hold of Jesus and let His Word change our lives. Trying to explain the relationship with

Jesus using mere words falls short of the reality. But if you let Him into your life, you will experience the change. It may not happen overnight, and circumstances will not always be perfect. But with Jesus and the salvation He brings, you will be equipped to handle the difficult things of life and even become a better person for them.

The greatest voice I have ever heard is Jesus' voice. To know that He is speaking to us is both exhilarating and humbling. Sometimes I have cried and begged Him not to be silent, though I know He is always with me. Hearing His voice makes Him seem nearer. There is an intimacy and a love with Him that is incomparable to that with other men and women in my life.

When I first got saved, that is pretty much all I was, just saved. I was legalistic and harsh, judgmental and condemning. I was strict on what other people did and was a nitpicker on how others behaved. I was not living in the freedom that Jesus preached. We do not follow Christ out of obligation; we follow and obey Him out of deep love and devotion. We love Christ and devote our lives to Him because He is our Savior and proved His ultimate love to us by dying on the cross in our place. During the time of Christ, often a criminal was crucified with the charge against him placed above his head on the cross. In the book of Matthew, we see that Jesus' charge was that He claimed to be the King of the Jews, yet He was, He really was. However, His accusers still had it wrong. Jesus wasn't just King of the Jews, He was King over *everything*. You know, I really love Jesus because it should have been me up there on the cross, not Him. Sometimes I wonder: Which charge would have been placed on my cross? I had many against me.

The Apostle Paul says in Romans 1:16 "For I am not ashamed of the gospel, because it is the power of God that brings salvation to everyone who believes: first to the Jew, then to the Gentile." As we see in this verse, the gospel is much more than just a story of a man who died. The gospel is the power of God that enables us to become saved. The very nature of what Jesus did was power; it emanated the power of God. When we become saved, we use the power of what Jesus did on the cross to change our lives. If Jesus could defeat death, then we can overcome everything in our own lives that hinders us from being all that God calls us to be. Our God is *Jehovah-Mekaddishkem* which means "The Lord that Sanctifies You." Simply, this means "The Lord that purifies you or sets you a part." We aren't perfect, and I have learned that the blood of Jesus gives us grace and the ability to do better. God cleans us up and sets us on the right path.

As I say frequently in this book: Christ loves you! He died to show you the extent of His love, and rose to show you the power of it.

There is much more to say about salvation, I could give detail after detail. But I want to leave you with this: Jesus wants to save you from your issues so that you can walk alive in Him. He wants to forgive you, save you, change you, and deliver you from everything that is not like Him in your life. I am not a scholar, nor am I a theologian. Jesus is just the best thing that has ever happened to me, and I want to share Him with you. I love Him; I worship Him. He is truly the love of my life. He has healed me and is healing me. He has changed me and is changing me. I am nothing other than a young college student who loves Jesus, who wants others to experience the freedom He has given me. If you are a young adult, especially if you are single, let Jesus have these years. Let Jesus free you and take you to new heights and give you an exciting life.

I decided that I wanted my life to glorify Jesus. People should look at our lives as believers and see that we are on a chase after Him. I desire for Jesus to get all of the use out of me that He can, without any hindrances. I decided long ago that I wanted the beauty of God's Spirit and the power of His love in my life to be evident to others, not so that my ego can be puffed up. But the reason is so that Jesus can be glorified through me and others can see who He is and receive Jesus into their lives.

Have you ever seen someone rushing by and you think, "Wow, wherever they are going it must be important." That's how I want people to look at my life. I want my chase after Christ to show just how important, real, and powerful He is. I neither need nor wish for the glory, I want Jesus to get it all, and the only way He will get it is if I allow my life to be a platform for Him. It's not about me. It's all about Christ and I want young people to see the difference He makes in the life of a believer.

Salvation is a life commitment and journey. Give your heart and your life to Jesus, and you will never regret it. He will do for you what no other can do. Life will not always be perfect, but Jesus will be with you every step of the way. Let Him be the Lord over your life; let Him be in control of your life. I am a living testament to the goodness, faithfulness, and sincerity of our Lord Jesus Christ. If you would like to be saved, just read this prayer out loud to Him and mean it in your heart, then watch Jesus prove Himself in your life.

"Jesus, I admit that I am a sinner, and that I have sinned. I confess that You died on the cross for my sins and rose on the third day, defeating death, giving me the ability to live a new life in You. I believe in my heart that You are the Savior and I ask You to come into my life and change me. I ask You to free me from all bondage and to heal my wounds. I ask You to send your Holy Spirit into my life so that I may have the power to live a life pleasing to You. I thank you for salvation. In Jesus' Name, Amen."

If you sincerely said this prayer, congratulations! Welcome to the family of Christ. Get connected to a Bible-believing and Holy Spirit–guided church. Read God's Word daily and watch Jesus change your life. He will heal you, and you will be free and walk in everything He has called you to. You will experience an intimacy and love with Jesus that you never thought possible. Just stay consistent, no matter what happens in life, and connect yourself with others who can help you on your walk.

Afterword

My story may not be for everyone, but it is for someone. It may not touch everyone, but if it touches only one, I consider God's will to have been done. I'm not a professional on emotional and mental matters, but that's okay because I have the Holy Ghost; I have God's Spirit living in me. I may not have a degree in counseling, but I know the Counselor. He has saved me; He has changed and is changing me. I love Jesus Christ; He is the author and the finisher of my faith. It is in Him that I move, live, and have my being. He has delivered me and is delivering me. I can honestly say that today I am truly learning to walk in forgiveness, security, purity, love, and joy. Am I perfect? No. Do I make mistakes? Yes, of course. Do I have all of the answers? No, but I am friend to the One who does.

In some ways, I am still that wide-eyed little girl who yearned to help those in need. The world needs the authentic love of Jesus Christ. I have visited foreign countries, and have visited different cities in the United States, and I have seen extreme poverty. On my first trip outside of the United States, I traveled to Mexico. We traveled on a bus to Teotihuacán, Mexico, in order to view ancient ruins. As we traveled through the countryside, my eyes locked on something I had never seen: the mountains were covered in shacks. For miles I watched as sickly dogs wandered through seemingly desolate streets. Old clothes lines hung lazily from shack to shack. I wondered what life must be like for people living in such squalid conditions. Then, I saw the face of that little African girl I had seen so many years ago, flash through my mind. In Belize and then in France I saw more poverty. When I studied in France, I saw so many people living on the streets. They slept in garbage bags and made small living spaces out of trash and old cardboard boxes. People were rummaging through trash bins in order to eat the leftovers of a burger someone wasted because the fast food place from which they purchased the burger "put too much ketchup on it." Now, that little girl is an adult who met the true Helper, Jesus. My motive at that young age was not to spread the gospel of Jesus. I just wanted to spread love and help the needy. But now I have a kingdom purpose, with a kingdom agenda. My kingdom purpose is, by the power of the Holy Spirit, to help free those in bondage and spread the gospel of Jesus. I thank God that all things work together for the good to those who love Him, and to those who are called according to His purpose. All of the trials, hurts, let-downs, and disappointments are in God's hands. We are healed and changed by the blood of Jesus, His love, and His Word. Jesus heals every type of pain and sickness, and every type of trauma or violation we may face. His sacrifice on the cross cleanses it all and triumphs over it all. Where His Spirit is, there is liberty and we can be confident that the truth of the cross, changes our lives. Faith in Jesus Christ and a relationship with Him does not only give you the desire to succeed, but it causes you to succeed. Even when we walk with Christ, life may not always be perfect, but His love supersedes everything that could come our way. Therefore, with boldness and faith in the Living God, we can decree: "But He was wounded for our transgressions, He was bruised for our iniquities; The chastisement for our peace was upon Him, And by His stripes we are healed!"